Vagabonds of the Sky

A PHOTOGRAPHIC HISTORY OF
AMERICA'S BARNSTORMING
PILOTS & DAREDEVILS

BRUCE
McALLISTER

Right: A Colorado antiquer flyin, June 2004. ©Bruce McAllister

Half title page: Art Smith was a featured Gates Flying Circus pilot who also performed at the Panama Pacific International Exposition in San Francisco in 1915. He perished in 1926 while carrying the night air mail on the Chicago–New York run. San Francisco History Center, San Francisco Public Library

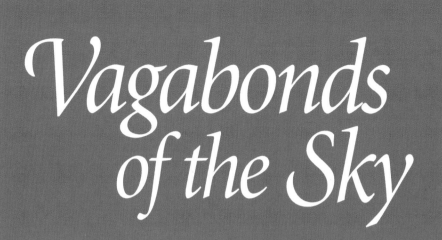

Vagabonds of the Sky

ROUNDUP PRESS

BOULDER, COLORADO, U.S.A.

In memory of those barnstorming pilots and daredevils who have broken the bonds of earth and taken us where eagles fly

Roundup Press, P.O. Box 109, Boulder, CO 80306-0109

Library of Congress Control Number 2004118276
ISBN 0-9638817-0-1

BOOK DESIGN
Paulette Livers, Livers Lambert Design, Boulder, CO

PHOTOGRAPHY EDITOR
Bruce McAllister

PHOTO CREDITS
Front Cover: ©Jim Koepnick/EAA
Back Cover: ©Mike Fizer

ACKNOWLEDGMENTS
Randy & Marion Acord, Pioneer Air Museum, Fairbanks
Noel Allard, Minnesota Aviation Hall of Fame
Christy Barden
Diane Bartels
Jack Greiner
Barbara Hansen, United Airlines Archives
Howard Ice
Bob Lentine
Dan Murray
Raymond L. Puffer, Ph.D., Historian, Edwards Air Force Base
Alan Renga, San Diego Aerospace Museum
Phil Simon
Robert O. Tyler
Flo Whyard
Richard Wien

DISCLAIMER
The author has attempted to give accurate aeronautical information. He cannot be held responsible for the accuracy of this information.

Also available from Roundup Press:
Wings Across America ISBN 0-9638817-9-5 $39.95 (Add $5.00 for P&H)
Wings Above the Arctic ISBN 0-9638817-8-7 $39.95 (Add $5.00 for P&H)
Wings Over the Alaska Highway ISBN 0-9638817-7-9 $34.95 (Add $5.00 for P&H)
Wings Over Denali ISBN 0-9638817-6-0 $29.95(Add $5.00 for P&H)

Printed & Bound in China by C & C Offset Printing, Ltd.

CONTENTS

INTRODUCTION

The world's first air show, hosted by France in 1909 in Rheims, was an extravaganza that attracted tens of thousands of European citizens and royalty. Aviation had become more than a curiosity to the world. The United States sent a Wright Flyer and a Curtiss pusher biplane, and France supplied four aircraft: a Farman, a Demoiselle, a Blériot XI, and a Voison. The Blériot XI caused a stir because Louis Blériot had just surprised the world by piloting that model aircraft across the English Channel. The main draw at Rheims was the air race. Glenn H. Curtiss challenged Blériot and all comers for the $100,000 purse. He backed up his words and beat Blériot by five seconds.

This air show established aviation as a major entertainment business—a true sport that continues to this day with air shows, large and small, all over the world. Barnstorming, which quickly caught on, would enhance these air shows with loops, spins, and daredevil acts. The Rheims air show grew into the Paris Air Show, which is still a premier aviation event.

One can argue that true aerobatic flying started in France in 1913 when a Frenchman, Adolphe Pégoud, unintentionally did a loop in his Blériot aircraft while experimenting with inverted flight and diving. The combined maneuvers described a circle. Not to be outdone by a Frenchman, Lincoln Beachey, an American stunt pilot, who was not impressed by the Frenchman's feat, came out of retirement to complete three loops. Beachey did not like to lose any competition—especially to a foreigner.

In the next decade, aerobatic flying came of age. Combat over Europe during World War I had created a surplus of well-trained young aviators. At

Aviation pioneer Glenn H. Curtiss, hailed by newspapers as Champion Aviator of the World in 1909, was a barnstormer at heart. He craved speed and set an airborne speed record of 46.5 miles per hour. In 1907, on a motorcycle, he set an unofficial world's record of 136.3 miles per hour. NASM-85-18299

An early air show poster.
Author's collection

the conclusion of the war, there were many unemployed pilots in North America with time to burn and the itch to fly. In the 1920s, with surplus military aircraft available, the veteran flyboys dreamed up what came to be known as "barnstorming"—a term adapted from theater lingo and applied to stunt flying in rural areas. These wild aerial demonstrations evolved into gypsy-like excursions through rural hamlets where locals, for a price, could have a spine-tingling aerial experience.

The most common surplus plane around was the Curtiss Jenny JN-4. Because Jennys were forgiving aircraft, they were perfect for barnstorming. If one collided with a haystack or a tree, the pilot would probably survive with perhaps only a bloody nose. The Jenny did not need much of a field to land and had a slow landing speed. And it was not expensive to repair. In the crate, a surplus Jenny cost only $200.[1] The OX-5 engine cost about $75, and surplus wings went for as little as $25 each.

An early 1900s Buick Sportster racing against an early model Curtiss pusher on a Florida beach, circa 1911. Florida State Archives

Bill Lindley was one of the early barnstormers in Florida. Florida State Archives

Opposite: In 1915, this army Curtiss Jenny made a spectacular landing on this tree. Usually, the most serious injury was to the pilot's ego. Florida State Archives

COMPLIMENTS OF
-FLOHRI- MISS HARRIET QUIMBY
-1911-

The arrangements for barnstorming shows followed a typical (although rather impromptu) pattern. A pilot or group of pilots would fly over a small town at low altitude and attempt to stir up an audience. They would then land at a local farm and negotiate with a farmer for use of one of his fields for an airstrip.

After the farmer gave his blessing and asked the pilots for some sort of compensation (such as money or a ride, which cost as little as $1 a person), the barnstormers would then "buzz" the town again, this time dropping handbills to get the word out. Many communities would declare a local holiday

Harriet Quimby became America's first licensed female pilot in 1911 and later joined the Moisant International Exhibition Team as a featured pilot. In 1912, she also became the first female pilot to fly across the English Channel—a trip that was considered extremely dangerous and death-defying at that time. Before her untimely death at an air meet in Massachusetts later that year, she reportedly had signed a $100,000 contract for an air show. For her performances, she always wore this trademark purple flying suit and her lucky jewelry. NASM-72-10099

and all work would stop when the barnstormers showed up.

As barnstormers perfected their routines, wing walkers (sometimes known as aerialists) enhanced the shows. The wing walkers wore winged costumes, parachuted, and made midair transfers. Perched on the wings of the aircraft, they would play tennis, dance, fence, and practice target shooting. There was no limit to what the aerialists could dream up.

Eventually, flying circuses evolved. Several aircraft and aerialists would book a specific event

Wing Walking by Sgt. Wells. Post Field, June, 25, 1922

Sergeant Wells did some spectacular wing walking at Post Field, Oklahoma, on June 25, 1922.
©San Diego Aerospace Museum

An army air show program celebrating the end of World War I, November 12–13, 1918. The show included a flying circus, aerial combat, and a parachute jump for a world's record. Commanding officer of Love Field, Major Albert L. Sneed, originated the Flyin' Frolic idea. Proceeds of the show went toward construction of recreational facilities for the pilots. **Courtesy Dan Murray**

Flyin' Frolic —
Love Field
Dallas, Tex.
Nov. 8-9

ahead of time. Ivan Gates, Jimmy Angel, Jessie Woods, and Douglas Davis started some of the best-known circuses. Gates started the $1-a-ride tradition, and Bill Brooks, one of his pilots, "broke all records by flying 980 passengers in a single day at Steubenville, Ohio."[2] Chief Pilot Clyde "Upside-Down" Pangborn rode herd over some of the best pilots in the world. Some experts speculate that the Gates Flying Circus turned out more famous pilots than the army and navy combined.

Women who worked in the barnstorming business in the 1920s were usually not pilots—they participated by wing walking, parachuting, and performing other aerial stunts. A black woman, Bessie Coleman, known "Queen Bess," ended that "tradition" when she overcame racial discrimination by hard work and perseverance. She became a real barnstormer. "Queen Bess" had a history of finding a way of achieving her goals. Although she did not have enough funds to finish college, she persisted in

Bessie Coleman was the first African American female pilot. She barnstormed in Los Angeles in 1923, after earning an international license in France. She became a role model for African Americans and women of all races. NASM-84-14782

pursuing her dream of becoming a pilot. Having saved enough money from various jobs, including running a chili parlor and working as a manicurist in a barbershop, Coleman went to France for pilot training. (Flight schools in the United States had turned her down.)

After just seven months of flight training in the renowned Caudron Brothers' School of Aviation in Le Crotoy, France, she earned her international pilot's license in June 1921. She was the first black woman in the world to become a licensed pilot. With additional flight training in Paris, she eventually earned long overdue respect in the United States and flew in her first air show on September 3, 1922, at Glenn Curtiss Field in Garden City, New York.[3]

During the next four years, "Queen Bess" became a celebrity as she toured the United States and encouraged both black Americans and women to take up flying. Tragically, she died in 1926 in the crash of a Jenny in which she was a passenger; she was scouting jump locations for an air show. Her mechanic, William Wells, who was piloting the airplane at the time, lost control of the plane after a loose wrench jammed the flight controls.

Before he made his famous trans-Atlantic flight, Charles Lindbergh had been a barnstormer.

In 1923, he bought his first plane (a war surplus OX-5-powered Jenny) in Miami and almost overnight became a barnstormer. On one occasion, he flew through what some fellow pilots described as the "worst flying country in the south." It was Lindbergh's first solo cross-country flight. Working his way through Mississippi, he started taking people

Charles Lindbergh barnstorming in the Midwest in the 1920s with his friend Harlan "Bud" Gurney. **United Airlines Archives**

for joy rides in Meridian and Maben. In Maben, over a period of two weeks, he carried sixty people for rides and took in $300. Because he did not have much aerobatic training, some of his dives and loops were just as exciting for him as they were for his rookie passengers. On one trip, Lindbergh "climbed to three thousand feet and started to fulfill my agreement [with the passenger] by doing a few air splashes, steep spirals and dives. … my passenger had his head down on the floor of the cockpit but continued to wave the red handkerchief with one hand while he was holding on to everything available with the other."[4] On another occasion, an elderly woman came up to Lindbergh and asked, "Boss! How much you all charge foah take me up to Heaben and leave me dah?"[5] Little did his passengers realize that they were getting rides with the man who was to become one of the most famous pilots of all time.

Above: Carl "Poochy" Smith being attended to after an accident near Oakland, California. He was one of the first stunt men to attempt a ground-to-air pickup. Unfortunately, it did not work, and he was dragged a considerable distance on the seat of his pants. ©San Diego Aerospace Museum

Opposite: Unidentified wing walker (maybe Gladys Ingle) making racecar-to-Jenny transfer in 1920s. ©San Diego Aerospace Museum

In 1919 Fred McCall landed this Curtiss Jenny JN-4 on a merry-go-round at the Calgary Stampede when he had engine trouble. Glenbow Archives, Calgary, AB, NA-1451-27

Opposite: Bill Lindley and wife at Daytona Beach, Florida, in 1919. Florida State Archives

But by 1927, the government introduced new safety regulations in response to numerous aircraft accidents. And the newly formed airlines and private pilots wanted "safer" skies as well. The new regulations were hard on the fragile Curtiss Jennys—they could not meet maintenance specifications on the ground or in the air. And the military had run out of its supply of surplus Jennys anyway.

The last straw came when the government cracked down on low-level aerial stunts. In 1936, it forbade wing walking below 1,500 feet. No longer would crowds get an intimate look at hair-raising dives, loops, and wing walkers. For aerialists (wing walkers and parachutists), insurance premiums went through the roof almost overnight. But in the golden age of the 1920s, the American public had a brief chance to see some of the best pilots do the best death-defying stunts—ever!

In this photographic history, the author has attempted to include a representative cross-section of barnstormers, living and deceased. He regrets his inability to include many great barnstormers, parachutists, and wing walkers who also deserve recognition. In most cases, however, there is simply not enough historical photography to document their considerable accomplishments.

One barnstormer best summed up his flying career in these sad but memorable words:

I can not do the old things now
That I've been used to do.
I'm all smashed up from doing stunts
And so must keep from view.
In doing tailspins near the ground,
I lost my nerve for sport.
I'm not good for anything—
One leg's a trifle short ..."[6]

CHAPTER 1

Lincoln Beachey: The Aerobatic Daredevil

Few aviation history buffs today remember the name Lincoln Beachey—but that's only because he did not live beyond his mid-twenties and died before the Golden Age of aviation. Lincoln Beachey was arguably the world's most skilled aerobatic pilot prior to World War I.

Born in San Francisco on March 3, 1887, Beachey, like the Wright brothers, developed an early interest in bicycles and by the age of 15 was repairing motorcycle engines. By age 18, he had helped Captain Thomas Scott Baldwin build the dirigible *California Arrow*. Baldwin was a bit too old and overweight to do his own flying, so he needed a pilot to fly his dirigible. Beachey became hooked on flying and soon he acquired his own dirigible and took it to the nation's capital. There he flew it around the Washington Monument, the Mall, and even touched down on the White House lawn.

By 1910, Beachey could see that fixed-wing aircraft were coming into vogue and dirigibles were on the wane. He started taking flying lessons at the Curtiss Flying School. Beachey was a stubborn,

Lincoln Beachey on one of his flybys, circa 1913. Location unknown. ©San Diego Aerospace Museum

In a Curtiss pusher, Lincoln Beachey made the first indoor airplane flight at the Palace of Machinery, during construction of the Panama Pacific International Exposition in San Francisco. **San Francisco History Center, San Francisco Public Library**

sometimes reckless student and crashed a few of Curtiss' aircraft. But Curtiss could see that Beachey had the necessary skills and hired him to do stunt-flying for his exhibition team. During his performances, Beachey relished doing a vertical climb until the aircraft stalled, which he followed by an exciting dive back toward attentive crowds. Only at the last possible moment did he pull out of the dive—usually close to the ground.

Beachey liked to show off and to enhance his image; always well dressed, he typically wore coat, tie, and a belted jacket. To complete his outfit, Beachey usually wore a tweed cap that gave him a rakish look. He had a soft spot for comely women and rumor had it that he carried diamonds around, promising every new female acquaintance that she had a special place in his heart!

In 1911, at the Chicago International Aviation Meet, he set a fixed-wing, high-altitude record

Lincoln Beachey making a loop over the Exposition grounds in San Francisco in 1915. San Francisco History Center, San Francisco Public Library. Inset: *An informal portrait of Lincoln Beachey with his Little Looper aircraft.* ©San Diego Aerospace Museum

Opposite: On June 26, 1911, Lincoln Beachey flew under the Honeymoon Bridge at Niagara Falls after he had awed thousands by flying through the mist near Horseshoe Falls. Niagara Falls Library, Niagara Falls, Ontario

by making a steep climb to 11,642 feet. At that point his aircraft ran out of fuel and he piloted it back to his starting point, making a dead-stick landing. To further build his reputation, Beachey was the first pilot to fly over Niagara's Horseshoe Falls and under nearby International Bridge.

In 1913, Beachey flew the first loop-the-loop maneuver in North America. He did this stunt more than 1,000 times, steadily increasing the number of consecutive loops on subsequent flights. He was determined to outdo his European counterparts like Frenchman Adolphe Pégoud, who was thought to be the first pilot to fly an aircraft upside down as well as the first to perform a loop on September 1, 1913. Beachey was not about to let a Frenchman steal his thunder!

Later, the European press learned that Pégoud was in fact not the first person to do a loop. Earlier "an obscure Russian military pilot named Peter Nesterov, out for a joy ride, had impulsively done the same stunt—and had been promptly put under house arrest for endangering government property."[1]

C. Adolphe Pégoud before his death in World War I. To the French, he was known as Le Roi de l'Air. *©S.H.A.A.*

In 1914, about 17 million Americans saw Beachey fly his Little Looper on a 126-city tour, and he was given the title Alexander, The Great of the Air.[2] His daily "firsts" were comparable to Lindbergh's well-publicized return from his epic trans-Atlantic crossing.

Beachey's accomplishments included the following firsts: inventing stall recovery, flying straight down, flying indoors, flying upside down, mastering the loop, tail-sliding (on purpose), and doing the barrel roll.

Beachey raced many sportscar drivers during his famous cross-country tour in 1914. Barney Oldfield was one of his "victims." ©San Diego Aerospace Museum

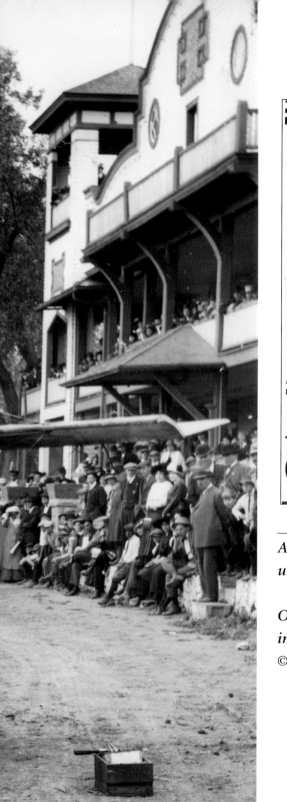

The Al Bahr Temple Shriners Announce Their Great **Sky Jubilee**

FIRST PUBLIC EXHIBITION

The Astounding Wizard of the Air

BEACHEY

The man who toys with fate—Upsets the laws of gravity and makes faces at the positive scientists.

LOOPING THE LOOP and Flying **UPSIDE DOWN**

IN addition, he will perform for one and one-half hours the most startling, most amazing and most spine-chilling low flying stunts ever witnessed—racing at 80 miles an hour against a giant racing automobile. The first hour of the flying program will consist of flying feats a few inches off the ground.

YOU must be inside the grounds to keep from CHEATING YOURSELF out of your life's greatest sensation. Gates open at 1 p.m.
Concert by Al Bahr Shriners' Band, commencing at 2:20 p.m.
Beachey's wonderful aeroplane on exhibition—attended by a lecturer—from opening of gates until he uses it. Ten-minute Ferry service, beginning at 1:20 p.m.

FLYING FROM 3 TO 4:30 P. M.---NO LATER

Admission 50c, Children 25c   Tickets on Sale at Street Ry. Office, Union Bldg

Coronado Polo Grounds Thanksgiving Day [TOMORROW

Above: A flyer promoting one of Beachey's exhibitions near San Diego. Date unknown. ©San Diego Aerospace Museum

Opposite: In Denver, a large ground crew helped Beachey turn his Little Looper into a strong wind for takeoff. At the time he was on a national tour. ©San Diego Aerospace Museum

Lincoln Beachey waves goodbye to crowds as he embarks on his fatal flight in San Francisco on March 14, 1915. ©San Diego Aerospace Museum

Opposite: Beachey and his collapsed Taube airplane falling into San Francisco Bay, March 14, 1915. The wings of his Taube separated at 500 feet above the water while he was in a steep dive. He died from injuries sustained in this accident. San Francisco History Center, San Francisco Public Library

Lincoln Beachey getting ready for a flight at the Iowa State Fair during his 1914 national tour. His mechanic, Warren Eaton, is at his side and Art Mix in the rear is about to prop the aircraft. His Little Looper aircraft was powered by an 80-horsepower engine, which weighed just 205 pounds. With 145-pound Beachey and 40 minutes' worth of fuel and lubricant, the Little Looper weighed only 773 pounds. ©San Diego Aerospace Museum

By 1915, Beachey was at the apex of his flying career and was invited to do his show at the Panama Pacific International Exposition in San Francisco, home of the Golden Gate. There he did the first landing in a building. But on March 14, 1915, his luck ran out when the wings of his new aerobatic plane broke off while he was making a dramatic dive over San Francisco Bay. Beachey died just before he was to receive credit for his great contributions to aviation—a special gold medal from the Panama Pacific International Exposition. He drowned in front of 250,000 spectators, and San Francisco's telephone lines were tied up for a day. In remembering Beachey, William Randolph Hearst told Eddie Rickenbacker, "That's the end not of a man, but of an era."[3]

Aviation historians have been remiss in not giving Lincoln Beachey more credit for what he accomplished in a rather short flying career. Carl Sandburg, who was a relatively unknown poet in the early 1900s, echoed the sentiment of the day when he wrote the following tribute to Beachey.

To Beachey, 1912
Riding against the east
A veering, steady shadow
Purrs the motor-call
Of the man-bird
Ready with the death-laughter
In his throat
And in his heart always
The love of the big blue beyond

Only a man
A far fleck of shadow on the east
Sitting at ease
With his hands on a wheel
And around him the large gray wings
Keep and deal kindly, O wings,
With the cool, calm shadow at the wheel.[4]

Opposite: Beachey poses for photographer in his new Taube "Dove" aircraft at Ocean Beach, San Francisco. The cowling over the engine helped keep oil from blowing back into the pilot's face. ©San Diego Aerospace Museum

CHAPTER 2

The Mabel Cody Flying Circus

Mabel Cody, a niece of Buffalo Bill Cody, shared much in common with her famous uncle. This feisty acrobat started her own flying circus in the South in the early 1920s. Her original acts included dancing on wings, dramatic parachute jumps, and even once an attempt to transfer from a boat to a plane. She was beginning to encroach on the male-dominated barnstorming circuit in Florida and soon "crossed horns" with Doug Davis, who had established a strong foothold in Alabama and Georgia; Davis started a price war with Cody's circus. He even tried to lure her pilots away to his enterprise. She countered by flying into towns one day ahead of him. Then he would do the same to her and would

This wing walker should have been reclassified as a wing hanger. **Florida State Archives**

arrive at a town two hours before she did.

Mabel Cody's roster included ex-navy pilot Slim Culpepper and daredevil wing walker Bonnie Rowe. Rowe was one of the first aerialists to jump from one plane to another and to hang by his toes from a trapeze hanging from a plane. Once, to raise cash, Rowe put his parachute in hock. As the story goes, he and several of his buddies holed up in a hotel room and sewed together a makeshift

Louis "Buggs" McGowan, a member of the Mabel Cody Flying Circus, performed dramatic stunts such as this auto-to-aircraft ladder trick at Daytona Beach in 1921. He died only two years later at the age of 21. **Florida State Archives**

Louis "Buggs" McGowan starting his dramatic transfer at Daytona Beach. **Florida State Archives**

parachute in one night. It worked fine the next day until he was about ten feet off the ground, when it split apart and unceremoniously dumped Rowe on the ground.[1]

Perhaps Cody's most enterprising employee was announcer Curly Burns, who billed Cody's pilots as war heroes, whether or not they had ever served in the military. He would feature a different pilot in every show, dressing that pilot to the hilt and then have him fly a more dramatic flight than his cohorts. The idea was to create hero images and build up their press. Handbills and posters would reinforce this. Referring to the crowds, Burns said, "The suckers … go big for that officer stuff."[2]

Mabel Cody's Flying Circus planned its arrival at various towns with military precision. The planes would mass and fly right over the selected town "on the deck"—or just above rooftops. Then the tight formation would split apart like a Roman candle and return to buzz Main Street and do lazy-eights. To top off this almost intimidating invasion, one plane would toss out a "body." The stunned townspeople would rush to the "body," only to discover it was a dummy, with handbills attached, urging them to come out and see a real performance.

Rumor has it that once Cody's and Davis's two flying circuses met over a small town and had a one-hour mock air battle.[3] Davis eventually won business away from Cody, but only because he took better care of his planes. Finally, the two ended the long competition and joined forces. Sometime later, Curly Burns pulled off the deal of deals and signed the combined flying circuses to a contract with the Curtis Candy Company. They renamed the new operation the Doug Davis Baby Ruth Flying Circus.

But the era of the vagabond flier was coming to a close quickly. The government was tightening

Opposite: Mabel Cody with some of her motoring friends. **Florida State Archives**

up on maintenance of the barnstorming planes. Aircraft engines had a finite lifespan, and new regulations required them to be maintained to a certain standard and overhauled after so many hours of service. In addition, the aerial circuses were getting bad press, and air carriers wanted to eliminate them—and to have the skies to themselves. Aviation had become "respectable."

Just a few years later, in 1934, Doug Davis missed a pylon turn at the Cleveland Air Races and died doing what he liked best—flying. Mabel Cody had lost her newfound friend, business partner, and confidant, Doug Davis.

Some Florida beauties pose with pilot on his amphibian. Date unknown. Author's collection

Opposite: *Thousands of people attended the Mabel Cody Flying Circus on weekends.* Florida State Archives

CHAPTER 3

The Gates Flying Circus

ounded by Major Ivan R. Gates in 1922, the Gates Flying Circus was arguably the most famous barnstorming group in North America. According to some historians, Gates produced more famous pilots than the military. The lineup included such greats as Didier Masson, Art Smith, Clyde "Upside Down" Pangborn, and Diavalo, Daredevil of the Air, the name taken by many aerialists who played a role created by Gates. Gates, a pre–World War I promoter of exhibition flights, "talked more people off the ground than anyone else."[1] He was the ultimate announcer. He envisioned the

Opposite and above: Clyde Pangborn attempts to transfer from a Lozier auto to a Curtiss Jenny at Silver Strand Beach, near San Diego, California, in 1920. Unfortunately, he lost his grip on the ladder and made a hard landing on the beach. His partner, Ralph Reed, was piloting the Jenny. ©Washington State University Library/San Diego Aerospace Museum

draw of air shows in the United States and did shows in every state.

Clyde E. Pangborn was part-owner of the operation as well as its chief pilot. He was noted for his "upside down" flying and for changing planes in midair. As a U.S. Army student pilot in 1918, Pangborn had learned about aerobatic flight early—and inadvertently—when he went into a spin on his first solo flight. His flight instructor, Max Miller, a famous air mail pilot, had warned him to reverse the controls if that happened. Luckily, "Pang" (as he was nicknamed), remembered to kick hard opposite rudder and push the stick forward to recover from the spin. He went on to become a flight instructor at Ellington Airfield near Houston, Texas. In 1924, he rescued Rosalie Gordon, an aerialist, who, during a jump, became snagged when her parachute got tangled in the landing gear of Pangborn's plane.

As World War I was drawing to a close, Pangborn and his friend Ralph Reed would often take flights, off-duty, in Pangborn's personal Curtiss Jenny, joyriding across the country. "They buzzed the stenographers in Houston office buildings and strafed the corrals of Texas ranches. They tried to take the knobs off the tops of flagpoles or fly low

Opposite: Didier Masson, a featured Gates Flying Circus pilot, later introduced stunt flying to western Canada. Glenbow Archives, Calgary, AB, NA-463-12

Right: Art Smith was a featured Gates Flying Circus pilot who also performed at the Panama Pacific International Exposition in San Francisco in 1915. He perished in 1926 while carrying the night air mail on the Chicago—New York run. San Francisco History Center, San Francisco Public Library

enough to set their watches by the big town hall clocks.[2] When the number of their aircraft was reported to the authorities, the two intrepid aviators bought some paint and altered the plane's registration number. Despite these aerial capers, Pangborn became one of Gates's safest pilots; over the years, he flew about 125,000 passengers without serious injury. Overall, the Gates Flying Circus had a fine safety record. From 1922 to 1928, the group flew more than one million passengers on joy rides without a fatality.

Left: Clyde Edward Pangborn was perhaps San Diego's most notorious stunt pilot. He was known for flying upside down, which was tricky in a Curtiss Jenny because it was difficult to keep the fuel flowing when the plane was upside down. ©San Diego Aerospace Museum

Opposite: Clyde Pangborn attempts to transfer from a Lozier auto to a Curtiss Jenny at Silver Strand Beach, near San Diego, California in 1920. Unfortunately he lost his grip on the ladder and made a hard landing on the beach. His partner, Ralph Reed, was piloting the Jenny. ©San Diego Aerospace Museum

THE AERIAL ACROBAT
"AIRDEVIL" CLYDE C. PANGBORN

Will stage a stunt absolutely new in aerial history--a long chance never before taken by any living aviator.

A FULL SPEED CHANGE FROM A SPEEDING AUTO-MOBILE ON THE BEACH AT CORONADO TENT CITY TO A ROPE LADDER SWINGING FROM A DIPPING PLANE.

The spectacular and hazardous change will be pulled on the wide beach, in full view of the crowd on the Tent City board walk.

Coronado Tent City. May 16, at 2:45 P. M.

However, there were some casualties. Among them was parachutist Wes May, who died after he crashed into a eucalyptus tree during an air show at San Francisco's Presidio. Shortly after that tragedy, Ivan Gates had the idea of creating a fictitious aerialist, The Great Diavalo, who could be played by many wing walkers and parachutists. He coined the trade name in honor of an Italian who had looped a bicycle going down a three-hundred-and-sixty-degree track. As management noted, "If Diavalo gets killed, we just get another one."[3] The first aerial "guinea pig" was Freddie Lund, a former cowboy and rodeo rider. He was perfectly suited for the job and became the first of many Diavalos! Unfortunately, 16 out of the 28 pilots who flew for the Gates Flying Circus died in plane crashes—not a good statistic. The Gates stuntmen did not fare much better.

A wife of a former Gates pilot commented on what it was like to be married to a barnstormer. "He always spoke of a mistress of the sky whom all flyers chased after. It must have been something like that to lure so many up there and then smash them back down when she was through with them."[4]

Clyde Pangborn (left) and Colonel Roscoe Turner look over a model of a Boeing 247 aircraft. Both were charter members of the Quiet Birdmen, a select group of the who's who of aviation. Date unknown. National Archives

CHAPTER 4

Hollywood's Aerial War

In the late 1920s and into the 1930s, Hollywood re-fought World War I on celluloid. And the air war made an especially dramatic subject to complement (even surpass) traditional ground war movies. Former barnstormer pilots resurfaced as stunt pilots and flew realistic dogfights over the varied terrain of southern California. Great weather, mountains, and beaches made the ideal palette for aerial scriptwriters. The movies added to the legend of the World War I combat pilot as the fair-haired, fearless fatalist who lived for the present because tomorrow he would probably die in a spectacular way—if he did not walk away with the leading lady.

Waldo Pepper (played by Robert Redford) impersonates one of his heroes in a Hollywood production, recreating World War I action. ©San Diego Aerospace Museum

Right: Wings *movie poster.* Author's collection

Hell's Angels *and* Dawn Patrol *movie posters.* Author's collection

In 1925, a group of pilots, race car drivers, wing walkers, and cinema photographers formed the Thirteen Black Cats. This organization catered to the motion picture industry and established standard rates for specific maneuvers.

Crash ships (fly into trees, houses, etc.)	$1200
Loop with man standing on center section	150
Loop with man on each wing, standing up	450
Ship change	100
Upside down ship change	500
Change–airplane to train	150
Change–automobile to train	150
Change–speedboat to airplane	250
Change–motorcycle to airplane	150
Parachute jump	80
Parachute races—two jumpers	150
Parachute jump—ocean-landing	150
Double parachute jump—two men, one parachute	180
Fight on upper wing—two men, one knocked off	225
Upside down flying	100
Upside down flying with one man on landing gear	150
Delayed opening parachute—over 1000 feet	150
Crash automobile into train	150
Head on collision with automobiles	250
Plane goes into spin to crash	1200
Plane spins down on fire, does not crash	50
Blow up plane in midair, pilot chutes out	1500[1]

Some of the Black Cats earned negative publicity when they buzzed a football game at the Los Angeles Coliseum. A story in the *Los Angeles Times* on October 31, 1926, described the stunt.

Three young "flying fools" in an airplane menaced the lives of 79,000 spectators yesterday between halves of the Stanford–USC football game at the Coliseum.

The three, pilot "Bon" MacDougall, "Fronty" Nichols and "Spider" Matlock, all members of the Thirteen Black Cats, began stunting over the Coliseum during the half-time entertainment.

As thousands shrank back in their seats, a plane swooped low with Matlock and Nichols standing on the wings.

It barely cleared the peristyle end of the stadium.

Spectators in the topmost seats were so close to the plane, they could distinguish the features of the fliers."[2]

The football fans were unaware that during the display, the airplane's radiator failed and fouled the spark plugs. The Thirteen Black Cats barely made it

In 1925 this group of Los Angeles-based stunt pilots banded together and formed a company named "The 13 Black Cats." From the movie production companies they demanded set prices for an extensive list of aerial stunts and considered their company's name good luck.
©San Diego Aerospace Museum

Opposite: Frank Tomick, pilot, and an unidentified cinematographer prepare to film an aerial sequence in the movie Hell's Angels.
©San Diego Aerospace Museum

FRANK TOMICK
PILOT

E. BURTON STEENE
"HELL'S ANGELS" "NOW WE'RE IN THE AIR"
"WINGS" "LEGION OF THE CONDEMNED"

out of the stadium intact. After that episode, the three lucky "flying fools" landed in a vacant lot near the stadium and attended the second half of the game.[3]

Despite such negative press, the Thirteen Black Cats did much of the stunt flying for the movies *Wings* and *Hell's Angels,* establishing themselves as aerial daredevils. Their fame spread as the epics won awards. In 1927, *Wings* flew away with the Academy's Best Picture Award.

The cost of making these films began to climb. In 1928, Howard Hughes bankrolled *Hell's Angels.* But talking films such as Howard Hawk's *Dawn Patrol* set the bar even higher, and suddenly movie budgets went sky-high. The production budget for *Hell's Angels* was $4 million. The film is memorable for its incredible footage of World War I aerial dogfights. Howard Hughes stopped at nothing to get every scene just right. He even flew one of the

Opposite: Pilots employed for the filming of Hell's Angels pose for a photo at Oakland Airport in 1928. According to information on the back of the photo, the aircraft is a Sikorsky bomber (maybe the Ilya Mourometz series), which flew in World War I. ©San Diego Aerospace Museum

A Fokker in action during filming of Hell's Angels. ©San Diego Aerospace Museum

Opposite: In the movie Wings, *thousands of troops from Fort Sam Houston, Texas, were recruited to recreate the World War I advance to Saint-Mihiel, France. Army engineers built a $300,000 replica of the Western Front at Camp Stanley, near San Antonio, Texas. Airborne and ground-level cameras covered several angles of this expensive scene.* ©San Diego Aerospace Museum

In this dramatic sequence in the filming of Wings, *stunt pilot Dick Grace crash-landed a Fokker D.VII and lived up to his reputation as "the crash king of Hollywood." Grace suffered whiplash in this sequence, and the next day his doctor declared that he had broken his neck.* ©San Diego Aerospace Museum

aircraft in the movie, injuring himself. Three pilots lost their lives during the filming. The big star of the movie was a relative unknown at the time—Jean Harlow. She played the role of a liberated woman who made fast work of vulnerable male pilots. The movie was the beginning of her overnight climb to stardom in Hollywood. Although the movie started out as a silent film, it was converted into a talking picture and was also one of the first movies to be subsequently color-tinted.

Dawn Patrol, originally produced in 1930, was so popular that it was remade in 1938 with Errol

An aerial sequence from the filming of Hell's Angels. ©San Diego Aerospace Museum

In this 1938 remake of Dawn Patrol, *three modified Nieuport 28 aircraft and three Thomas Morse Scout fighters (in rear) get ready for takeoff. Errol Flynn is the pilot in the Nieuport (foreground).* ©San Diego Aerospace Museum

Before the filming of an aerial dogfight in the movie Hell's Angels, *pilots get a thorough briefing in front of a blackboard.* ©San Diego Aerospace Museum

©San Diego Aerospace Museum

Flynn as the lead actor, playing a pilot in the forward French headquarters of a British Royal Flying Corps unit, the 59th division. The ruthless squadron commander (played by Basil Rathbone) is accused of sending his young pilots on suicidal missions over enemy lines. David Niven played the role of Flynn's younger brother (also a pilot); his character is killed in action during one of the controversial missions.

In 1975, Universal Pictures came out with the ultimate barnstormer movie—*The Great Waldo Pepper*. Robert Redford played Waldo Pepper, a biplane pilot who misses the action of World War I and the excitement of being a combat pilot, boring holes through the sky as he skirmished with the German aces. Pepper and a friend, air show entrepreneur Axel Olsson (played by Bo Svenson), start a barnstorming business, taking people for short rides and entertaining them with wing-walking stunts. Eventually, Pepper and his partner get into trouble for dangerous stunts, and a young woman (played by Susan Sarandon) dies as she "freezes up" doing a wing-walking stunt. Pepper and his partner then lose their air show permit, give up their fledgling business, and go to Hollywood where Pepper can live out his World War I fantasies. One of the most impressive scenes of the movie is the dogfight that occurs between Pepper, who has a key role in a movie production (as a movie stunt pilot), and a former German ace, Ernst Kessler (played by Bo Brundin). The audience naturally assumed that the skirmish was make-believe, but in fact it was a real dogfight. The only thing missing was live ammunition.

When director George Roy Hill was asked how lead stunt pilot Frank Tallman protected himself in the crashes in *Great Waldo Pepper*, he replied, "He packs himself in Styrofoam and wears a steel brace and really straps himself down. He had scuba gear in the plane for the crash in the pond in case he flipped, and that could have been dangerous. Frank has a wooden leg, which doesn't help his mobility much, but he insists on doing all the really hairy crashes himself."[4] When asked which stunt was the most dangerous in the movie, Hill replied, "I think flying through the town was the most dangerous. We had to take down all the wires in the town in order

Hollywood's most versatile stunt pilot, Frank Tallman, could fly more makes and models of antique aircraft than any other pilot in the world. His book, Flying the Old Planes, *is a classic.* NASM-2004-60719

to do it, and get special permission from the FAA. The people in the street are stuntmen, and we had to evacuate the area for blocks around. Frank [Tallman] had only a couple of feet between his wing tips and the streetlight poles, and one gust of wind could have been disaster for him and part of the town. And anyone who has ever wrestled with flying a J-1 Standard knows the enormous skill and courage it took to thread that sluggish plane through the street."[5]

In his book, *Flying the Old Planes,* Tallman indicated that he still had a warm place in his heart for the Standard. "Looking back on my friendly years with the J-1 Standard is like peering into the rarely opened flight log of a barnstormer. I have landed in plow fields so rough only a Jeep could use them. I have sweated the first turn of a spin with a wing walker trying to get back from the cabanes [a mastlike structure for supporting wings]. I have worried through car-to-plane pickups from an open touring car, and I have flown in the sun, the rain, and the darkness."[6]

Over the years, Hollywood's stunt pilots proved to be among the very best pilots in North America. And of this group, Frank Tallman was the best. He could fly anything with wings.

Movie actor Charlie Chaplin (left) with Paul Mantz, one of the top stunt pilots to perform aerial sequences in World War I movies. ©San Diego Aerospace Museum

Opposite: Paul Mantz made a hair-raising pass through this hangar at Bishop, California, for Universal Pictures in the 1932 movie Air Mail. *In the movie, Ralph Bellamy and Pat O'Brien were the heroes.* ©San Diego Aerospace Museum

In the early 1960s, at Borrego Springs, California, movie stunt pilot Cliff Winters wowed the cameras as he crashed this pseudo-Messerschmitt Bf 109 into a building for a motion picture. NASM-91-1838

Opposite: Dick Grace proudly shows off an American Eagle aircraft he crashed in the filming of The Young Eagles. *Grace later admitted that this was the most violent stunt in his career—the force of the crash knocked the shoes from his feet. Buddy Rogers and Jean Arthur starred in the Paramount production, which was filmed in 1930.* ©San Diego Aerospace Museum

CHAPTER 5

Ernie "Ox" Boffa: Canadian Barnstormer

E rnest "Ox" Boffa was one of a kind: one of Canada's top barnstormer pilots and one of his country's most versatile pilots. "Ox" was also an aircraft mechanic, bush pilot, crop duster, and Arctic explorer.

He was born in Italy in 1904 and immigrated to Canada in 1907. His family eventually settled down in Fort William, Ontario, where Boffa secured part-time employment at a bicycle shop in 1915. He later worked as an apprentice with Canadian Car and Foundry while taking correspondence courses in mechanical engineering and two years of drafting

classes at night school. When the company closed, he found work as an auto mechanic and raced cars at local fairs. All the while he dreamed of flying.

Ernie moved to Great Falls, Montana, in 1927, where he pursued his dream by taking lessons at Vance Air Services. Because the company had a shortage of instructors, pilots from National Parks Airlines filled in

Opposite: Ernie Boffa, January 2002. ©Bruce McAllister

Poster highlighting Boffa's stunt flying. He participated in many such events in Montana and Minnesota. **Courtesy Flo Whyard**

Ernie "Ox" Boffa, pilot and barnstormer, at Lethbridge, Alberta, 1929. **Glenbow Archives, Calgary, AB, NA-3277-68**

when needed. As a result, Boffa had six different instructors for the nine hours that he needed to solo. While taking flying lessons, he also worked at an auto body shop, where he discovered the art of acetylene welding. Boffa learned aircraft wood and fabric work from the very man who prepared the wings and control surfaces of Lindbergh's *Spirit of St. Louis*.[1] These skills paid off when Boffa barnstormed.

In 1928, Boffa picked up his U.S. pilot's and mechanic's licenses. Then in 1929, he bought his first aircraft, a badly damaged Waco 10. It cost him $125 US. to restore. Shortly thereafter, he moved to Lethbridge, Alberta, where he landed a job with Southern Alberta Airways. When the company's Gypsy Moth was badly damaged, Boffa's Waco was used as a substitute while he rebuilt the Moth. The company produced the *Flying Frolics* and put on wild demonstrations of wing walking and parachute jumping at regional air shows.

Once Boffa played stuntman for fellow pilot Z. Lewis Leigh in what could have been a fatal role. In a beer parlor, they concocted what they thought would be an original stunt. Boffa was to appear to be hanging on to a rope attached to the undercarriage of the Waco without a parachute. (A steel safety snap attached to his harness and a wire connected him to the Waco.) However, after the stunt was completed, Boffa could not get back into the aircraft. The Waco would have to land with him in tow. As Leigh flared the aircraft gingerly, "[Ernie] was pumping his legs like crazy, bounding along in giant 30-foot strides behind the Waco. In the crowd there was pandemonium; more than one woman fainted. [After the landing] from under the plane crawled a figure in white flying overalls, dirty, somewhat bloodied about the knees, elbows, and nose. One woman then uttered the most appropriate words for the occasion: 'Come to my house and have a drink. You both deserve it.'"[2]

Ernie Boffa received his Canadian licenses in 1931, was engaged in crop dusting in Alberta, and eventually became one of Canada's top Arctic bush pilots. Before retirement, he flew pioneering flights to the far reaches of Canada's Arctic and participated in DEW Line Station construction support. The Canadian government, in recognition of his work, named a lake after him in the high Canadian Arctic.

In true barnstormer tradition, Boffa was fearless but he also was a jack-of-all-trades—mechanic, pilot, and survivalist. Before his death, Boffa was elected to Canada's Aviation Hall of Fame in 1993 and also earned the Yukon's prestigious Order of Polaris, an award reserved for very few pilots. He put in more than 26,000 hours as a pilot in command and until his death had a valid driver's license. He lived to within a few months of being one hundred years old when he passed away in 2003.

Frank "Wild Irish" Haddock (left) and Ernie Boffa at a parachute demonstration in Calgary. Glenbow Archives, Calgary, AB, NA-5467-47

CHAPTER 6

Noel Wien: Alaska's Pioneer Barnstormer

Noel Wien (1899–1977) put Alaska aviation on the map in 1924 when he flew the first non-stop flight between Anchorage and Fairbanks in a Hisso-powered Standard aircraft. But Wien had also done some barnstorming in Anchorage prior to his Fairbanks flight, introducing aviation to the people of Anchorage (who had built him an airfield so he could give rides to the public while he was preparing for his pioneer flight). Jimmy Rodebaugh, an enterprising railroad man in Fairbanks, had hired Wien to fly one of two Standards (which he had purchased outside Alaska) to be used for charter work out of Fairbanks.

Starting in 1925, Wien made several trips to the lower 48 states to pick up new aircraft and to get his brothers, Ralph, Fritz, and Sigurd, to move to Alaska. During that time, he also barnstormed for the Federated Flyers Flying Circus. During this stage of his life he perfected many of the flying skills and good judgment that would serve him well during his years of flying in Alaska.

Opposite: Noel Wien poses with two young women after a barnstorming ride over Anchorage in late June or early July in 1924. On July 6, he flew this Hisso Standard on the first flight between Anchorage and Fairbanks. **Courtesy Richard Wien**

Noel Wien with a Curtiss Jenny in the early 1920s. **Courtesy Richard Wien**

Above, left: Noel Wien (second from left) before participating in a motorcycle race at an air circus in the late 1920s. After participating in a few races, he discouraged his children from riding motorcycles. Courtesy Richard Wien

Above, right: Noel Wien demonstrating wing-walking technique to an unknown audience in the mid-1920s. At the time, he was working for the Federated Flyers. Courtesy Richard Wien

Opposite: Noel Wien with his Curtiss Jenny at Upper Sandusky, Ohio, in 1926. At the time, he was working for the Federated Flyers. Courtesy Richard Wien

A Minnesota native, Noel Wien became a barnstormer almost overnight in the 1920s, when a man named Edgar William Morrill gave him a chance to fly half of his passenger-carrying revenue hops, even though Wien did not yet have 50 hours of flight time—the minimum required for aircraft insurance. Wien displayed his potential as a natural-born pilot when he showed Morrill that he could land his dual-control plane in a short cornfield with more skill than veteran Morrill. Morrill's wife, who

Noel Wien took this twilight photo of some barn-storming aircraft between shows in the lower 48 states in the 1920s. He was a talented photographer. Exact location is unknown.
Courtesy Richard Wien

Opposite: Clarence Hinck and his parachuting girls. Although he was one of the best air show promoters in the United States in the 1920s, Hinck defaulted on a promise to get work for Wien in Mexico.
Courtesy Noel Allard

was the ticket manager, cook, and promoter for her husband, accompanied the two barnstormers on their trips. Working their way west, the Morrills and Wien used road maps as they extended their barn-storming operations into South Dakota and such exotic midwest towns as Clara City, Marshall, Verdi, Clear Lake, Red Field, and Stockholm.[1]

As they arrived in each town, they would usually buzz the main street before touching down in a suitable field—often a racetrack. Racetrack owners did not ask for a rental fee, whereas farmers usually expected some form of compensation for

use of their fields. Wien carefully evaluated each of his paying passengers and would not do elaborate stunts if he felt they wanted a more predictable ride. He was building valuable flight time and treated flying as his life's work, not just as a business.

Soon thereafter Wien found a job with the Federated Flyers (doing loops with wing walkers); he performed for large crowds. He also rode motorcycles as part of the act. After the aerial circus season ended in 1922, Wien signed on with Clarence Hinck, an agent for Mexican rebels who were looking for pilots to drop bombs on the opposing federal forces in the country's civil war. Wien went to New Orleans to await instructions from Hinck, but nothing in the contract materialized, and suddenly he was without

Noel Wien (left) with his Curtiss Jenny at Upper Sandusky, Ohio, in 1926. At the time, he was working for the Federated Flyers road show. Courtesy Richard Wien

Opposite: Noel Wien and friends in 1924 with a Boeing Model C-5 Series seaplane. This seaplane was difficult to fly (because of its flying tail), and after Noel Wien flew it a few times, a cocky World War I pilot crash-landed it on the mud flats. Two boys tried to salvage the floats to make a boat, but drowned in the attempt. This photo was taken at the Cook Inlet near Anchorage. Several C series aircraft were declared surplus by the U.S. Navy after World War I and at least two were painted German colors and crashed for the film Dawn Patrol *in 1931.* Courtesy Richard Wien

Noel Wien's Hisso Standard aircraft needed a helping hand after it bogged down on the airstrip in Circle Hot Springs, Alaska, in 1925. **Courtesy Richard Wien**

a job and without money. There was an aircraft in a crate at the depot, but he did not have enough money to pay the collect freight charges and at least claim the plane. The Mexican civil war was over, and Hinck had defaulted on his contract.

Things were not looking good for Wien, as he survived on a diet of bananas and hope. At that time, pilots "weren't considered much. People thought you might be all right or you might be crazy. They'd put up big picture-posters of you at county fairs, but nobody would give you a steady job."[2]

In 1924, things changed dramatically when Jimmy Rodebaugh, offered Wien a job in Fairbanks with a guaranteed salary of $300 a month—good money in those days, even in Alaska. With his old friend, mechanic Bill Yunker, Wien proceeded by steamer to Seward with a crated Hisso-powered Standard. Then by railroad they took the crated

Standard from Seward to Anchorage where they found a receptive audience and a dusty homemade field developed on a road and shared with cars. "The autos," he said, "were really no trouble at all. There was only my plane, and people were on the lookout for me."[3] Rodebaugh allowed Wien to barnstorm in Anchorage for several weeks as they modified the plane's fuel tanks to enable them to fly nonstop to Fairbanks. Wien took the locals on joy-hopping and sightseeing flights, making lots of money for his new employer. Alaskans got their first taste of barnstorming.

During his stay in Anchorage, Wien also flew one of the first Boeing seaplanes ever built. A local man named Hammontree had flown the Boeing C-5 seaplane to Anchorage in 1922 for an exhibition flight. After that, it had been stored in a warehouse until an adventuresome pilot, Al Jones, bought it. He discovered it was quite unstable and difficult to fly, and almost wrecked it. Because it had a flying tail, it was difficult to control. Noel Wien then tried his luck with the seaplane and flew it successfully seven times in June 1924. Then a veteran World War I pilot tried his luck with the seaplane and wrecked it. The floats were left on the Cook Inlet mud flats; some time later, two boys drowned while trying to salvage the floats. Alaska's first barnstorming seaplane had a short-lived and unlucky service life.[4]

Wien successfully pioneered many routes throughout Alaska in the years to come, and in 1924 he started charter service out of Fairbanks. With his brother Ralph he eventually created one of the best airlines in Alaska—Northern Air Transport, which eventually became Wien Alaska Airlines and finally Wien Consolidated Airlines. It ended operations in mid-1984, having celebrated 60 years of serving the people of Alaska.

Noel Wien's flying career in Alaska reflected much of what he learned as a barnstormer. "He has had his full share of luck. But it is more than this that saved him from the untimely death of fellow pilots. From the start he exhibited a remarkable faculty for doing daring things in a cautious way."[5]

Noel Wien introduced Marvel Crosson (right) to Alaska bush-flying in the 1920s before her untimely death in the lower 48 states while participating in a women's air race. This photo was taken in the Fairbanks area. **Courtesy Richard Wien**

Evelyn Sharp
Lincoln Flying School
May 1935
Lincoln, Nebraska

CHAPTER 7

Evelyn "Sharpie" Sharp: Nebraska's Barnstormer

During the Great Depression, a young girl by the name of Evelyn Sharp grew up in the north central region of the Nebraska sand hills. A very independent young person, Sharp was not looking for the security of a husband and a hearth. She dreamed of becoming a pilot and breaking the bonds of earth. As an orphan, she was adopted by a childless couple who moved often, but treated her well.

Evelyn was very active in sports at Ord High School and graduated in 1937, gaining honor as the best female athlete in the school's history. A flight instructor, Jack Jefford, who rented a room from her

parents and was behind in his rent, offered to give the young girl free flying lessons. Evelyn took her first flight when she was just fifteen years old and soloed one year later. Jefford went on to become one of Alaska's best bush pilots.

The Ord business community was impressed by Sharp's determination to become a great pilot and made a down payment on a new Taylor J-2 Cub for her use. In return, she promised to repay the community by advertising and promoting the North Loup Valley during her barnstorming trips. The business arrangement was good for both parties. Sharp earned her private license by age seventeen

---

Opposite: Evelyn "Sharpie" Sharp gets ready for instruction at the Lincoln Airplane & Flying School, Lincoln, Nebraska, in 1938. **Courtesy Diane Bartels**

Sharp revered her first flight instructor, Jack Jefford. He later became a legendary bush pilot in Alaska. Photo taken in November 1936, Ord, Nebraska. Courtesy Diane Bartels

Opposite: In January 1936, Sharp learned to fly near Ord, Nebraska, and made many of her early landings on the North Loup River (in center of this aerial photo), which was frozen at the time. Courtesy Diane Bartels

In 1936, at Ord, Nebraska, Sharp learned to fly in this Aeronca C-3, known as the "Flying Bathtub." Courtesy Diane Bartels

Opposite: In 1937, Evelyn Sharp was the first pilot to land at Arrasmith Field in Grand Island, Nebraska. Legendary Alaska pilot Joe Crosson (right) was one of the welcoming committee. Courtesy Diane Bartels

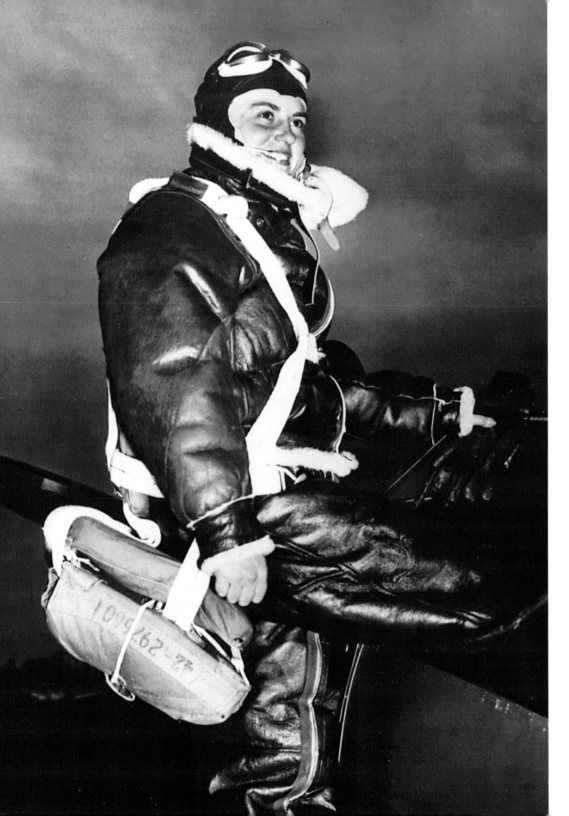

and her commercial license the following year. In 1938 and 1939, "Sharpie" made appearances at county fairs and community events, giving more than 5,000 people barnstorming rides. Many of her passengers had never been in an aircraft before.

In 1940, Harry E. Mendenhall wrote a poem that appeared in the Nebraska *State House News*. In it, he expressed Nebraska's admiration for its first and most famous aviatrix:

Evelyn Sharp

What eagle circles yonder lofty peak,
Now vanishing into the morning mist,
Now gliding earthward seemingly to seek
Some treasure its discerning eye had missed.

Ah, now the fog has lifted and I see
More plainly through the fastly clearing skies,
And smile to think I could mistaken be;
It's Evelyn in her morning exercise.

T'would seem her dauntless spirit cannot rest
Upon an ordinary couch of ease;
No doubt to her some feathery cloud is best,
So off she goes to race the morning breeze.[1]

By age twenty, Sharp was one of only ten women flight instructors in the United States. She gave flight instruction to more than 350 men in the U.S. government's pre–World War II Civilian Pilot Training Program in South Dakota and California. As her career accelerated, she was able to support her adoptive parents.

When the War Department organized the Women's Auxiliary Ferrying Squadron in 1942, Sharp was recruited as its seventeenth member. She had more flight hours than any other woman pilot at that time. Sharp flew nearly every airplane in the U.S. Army Air Force inventory: North American AT-6 Texans, Vultee BT-13s, Fairchild PT-19s, Douglas C-47s, Douglas A-20 Havocs, Martin B-26B Bombers, Mitchell B-25s, North American P-51 Mustangs, and Lockheed P-38 Lightnings. She was working on her Boeing B-17 rating when misfortune struck.

On April 3, 1944, on a P-38 Lightning ferry mission, she lost power in one engine on takeoff from New Cumberland, Pennsylvania. Although the aircraft crash-landed with little damage, the impact catapulted Sharpie through the canopy and she died instantly. Sharp perished doing what she loved best.

Every year the community of Ord, Nebraska, celebrates her memory with Evelyn Sharp Days. She was the first woman inducted into Nebraska's Aviation Hall of Fame and is probably its most famous woman pilot. The airport in Ord is named after her.

Sharp's career ended tragically in 1944. She was ferrying a Lockheed P-38 Lightning, when one engine failed on take-off. She was just twenty-five and had flown most of the military's aircraft inventory. **Courtesy Diane Bartels**

Opposite: Evelyn Sharp climbing aboard a Fairchild PT-19 Cornell *aircraft at the factory in Hagerstown, Maryland, prior to takeoff on a delivery flight in November 1942.* **Courtesy Diane Bartels**

CHAPTER 8

Clyde Ice: The Tri-motor Barnstormer

Considered one of South Dakota's greatest pilots, Clyde Ice (1889–1992) was arguably the state's most versatile and legendary pilot. He started his flying career in 1919 and flew approximately 40,000 flight hours in 54 years. In that period, he barnstormed, did charter work, flew air mail routes, piloted winter mercy missions, crop-dusted, and helped ranchers herd horses and hunt coyotes from the air. In addition, during World War II, he instructed 2,000 men in the Army Air Corps in primary flight training. At age 100, he was still operating a combine, even though he was no longer fly-ing. He was the first pilot inducted into the South Dakota Aviation Hall of Fame.

Ice had no use for pilots who liked to show off. During his career, he helped rescue fif-teen pilots from crashes. In almost every rescue, he recalled, the pilot had taken unnecessary risks. In his entire career, he never had a serious accident. Once his aircraft lost

Above, right: Clyde Ice at age 86 still had the passion to fly and had no concerns about passing his flight physical. **Courtesy Chuck Ice**

Opposite: In 1928, the Blackfoot Indians in Montana named Clyde Ice's Ford Tri-motor aircraft Wamblee Ohanko, *which means Swift Eagle.* **Courtesy Howard Ice**

Johnny Gisi (left) and Clyde Ice with one of Ice's early planes, a Lincoln Standard. Gisi was the parachutist at all the air shows both men participated in. Circa 1923. **Courtesy Howard Ice**

power as he was flying up a box canyon to help a rancher round up some horses. He landed among some big rocks, damaging the prop and landing gear. "I had to take the airplane apart, piece by piece and out of the canyon."[1] He also once ran into a haystack, but during his entire career never "totaled" an aircraft.

He thought that his pilot's license should have been one of the first 100 issued by the federal government instead of number 1,598. "The government only had about two license inspectors for the whole country back then," he said, "and every time one would come through where I was, I'd be out barnstorming. If it hadn't been for that, I'd be way under 100."[2]

In 1919, Ice's flying career commenced on a bumpy note. He had been selling tickets for barnstormer Earl Vance. "Well, we were going over to another town [on a barnstorming trip] and I knew there was a great big pasture over there. I was sure we could haul a lot of passengers. Earl put me in the back seat. … I had wiggled the stick a few times before and watched to see what happened, but I always figured you had to move it around like a pump handle. I was surprised to find out how little

it took. Well, we go there and I circled around to line up where I figured he'd want to land, and let the nose down some. He just reached over, shut off the gas and yelled: 'Land 'er, land 'er.' Well, I thought he must know what he's doing so I pointed it down. … Later he told the boys 'He landed alright but he made six [landings] in one, but I found out later that he needed the practice.'"[3]

After barnstorming with a Standard for many years, Ice and some partners formed Rapid Airlines, hoping to start an air mail run from a base in Omaha. He started using the slogan "Safe and Sane Flying." When the air mail contract never materialized, he tried to convince his partners to buy a Ford Tri-motor. When Ice was 38, the group bought Tri-motor Number 20 off the assembly line, and Ice flew off to do air shows and barnstorming. The Blackfoot Indians nicknamed the Tri-motor *Wamblee Ohanko*, which means Swift Eagle. He flew it all over the United States and took passengers on short rides at $5 apiece. One day "he hauled 510 passengers at $5 a head. He remembers that night in Buffalo, N.Y., when he had so much money in the plane that some men were waiting around to rob him when he quit work after midnight. The police

Clyde Ice's first Ford Tri-motor aircraft appeared at the Rapid City, South Dakota, Air Show in 1928.
Courtesy Howard Ice

Opposite: Clyde Ice with the chief of the Blackfoot Tribe in 1928. Chief Two Guns White Calf insisted on flying right seat on the first flight of the first Ford Tri-motor aircraft Ice owned. Courtesy Howard Ice

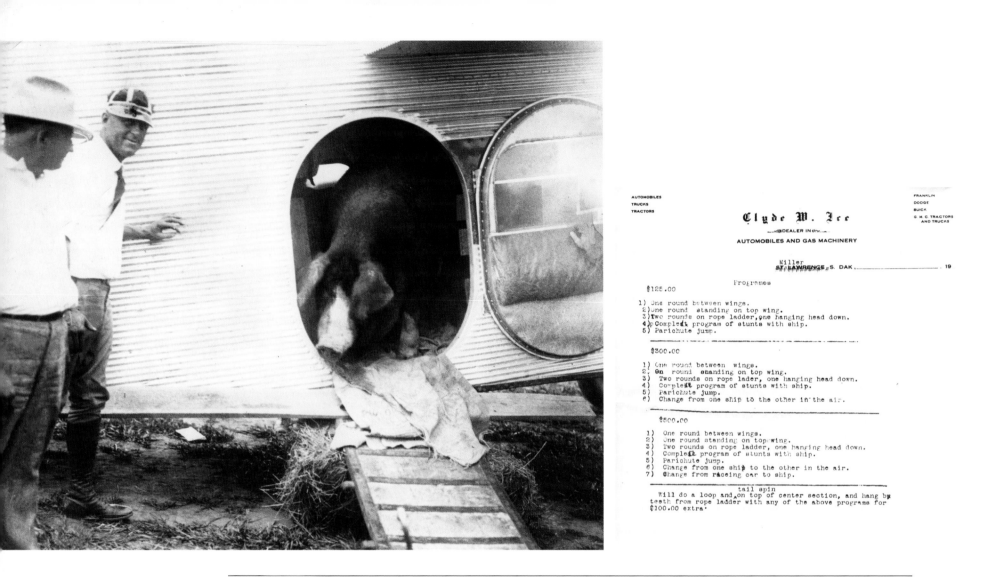

In his first Ford Tri-motor, Clyde Ice flew Dazzler, *a 1,220-pound pig, to Des Moines from Leigh, Nebraska, in 1928.* Courtesy Howard Ice

Above, right: Clyde Ice's barnstorming price list. Courtesy Howard Ice

waited, too, and gave him an armed escort into town."[4] In those days he sent an average of $1,000 a day back to his business partners; to make that much money, he tried to cover all the major cities, coast to coast.

For about five years, Ice barnstormed in the Tri-motor and drummed up additional business by flying at night and selling rides at a penny a pound. He also went barnstorming in Mexico for two winters. Working the Yucatan region, he ran afoul of some local bandits when he turned down repeated requests to use the Tri-motor to haul their heavy guns. Whenever he saw a cloud of dust erupt near where he based his Tri-motor, Ice knew it was bandit cavalry on a surprise visit. He would promptly take off before they could corner him, his crew, and his beloved Ford Tri-motor.

Clyde Ice set the bar for South Dakota pilots, and the Spearfish, South Dakota, airport is named in his honor.

Clyde Ice (right) with an aircraft guard at Mexico City, November 1928. **Courtesy Howard Ice**

CHAPTER 9

Pancho Barnes: The Hollywood Barnstormer

Florence "Pancho" Barnes was one of the most memorable of America's pioneering women stunt pilots. Born into wealth on July 14, 1901, she grew up in a 32-room mansion near Pasadena, California. She took to riding horses, hunting, and the outdoors. Her grandfather took her to her first air show when she was nine, and soon planes replaced horses as her primary passion.

A "proper" marriage to an Episcopal priest and the subsequent birth of a son, William, did not fit in with her goals or her personality. By 1928, she had abandoned her family and signed on a freighter to Mexico—as a man! She then roamed Mexico's unstable, revolution-prone interior, traveling in the company of a wayward seaman. Her companion nicknamed her "Pancho," noting her resemblance to Don Quixote's sidekick as she rode a donkey cross-country. That nickname stuck for the rest of Barnes's life—it fit her personality to a "T."

Returning to California later that year, Barnes decided to try her hand at flying. Lindbergh had just flown across the Atlantic, and everybody was excited about aviation. She bought an OX-5-powered Travel Air aircraft, hired an instructor, and

---

Opposite: The first supersonic test pilots at Edwards Air Force Base set up "headquarters" at Pancho Barnes's bar, where they did not have to worry about base regulations. They could exchange war stories, drink, and enjoy themselves. Gus Askounis (left) at the piano, Jack Ridley, Ike Northrup, Peter Everest, **Pancho, Chuck Yeager, and an unidentified pilot. History Office, Air Force Flight Test Center**

This portrait (by photographer George Hurrell) might be the best ever taken of Pancho Barnes. Barnes liked his photography so much that she introduced him to her Hollywood friends, and he landed a job as MGM's chief still photographer. History Office, Air Force Flight Test Center

Pancho Barnes with her Travel Air Model R aircraft, known as Mystery Ship because the manufacturer kept its development under "wraps." The aircraft had a top speed in excess of 200 miles per hour. History Office, Air Force Flight Test Center

soloed after six hours of instruction. She was hooked on aviation and it became her passion.

In line with her maverick personality, Pancho started wearing men's clothes, smoking cigars, and using four-letter words. She started the Pancho Barnes Mystery Circus of the Air and began barnstorming cross-country.

Within only one year of earning her pilot's license, Barnes joined nineteen other women to fly in the 1929 Women's Air Derby, an air race from Santa Monica, California, to Cleveland, Ohio. In what became known as the Powder Puff Derby, Pancho had bad luck and collided with a truck on the runway at Pecos, Texas. She was not injured, but her plane was grounded for repairs.

Union Oil Company was impressed with Barnes's high-profile flying and soon signed her to a three-year contract doing demonstration flights and promotional work; in return, Union Oil sponsored her

Pancho Barnes was a close friend of Ramon Novarro, who was a leading actor at MGM in the roaring twenties. Hollywood stars would often play as well as work at Pancho's ranch. Test pilots would then find an excuse to drop by. **History Office, Air Force Flight Test Center**

On August 18, 1929, the top women pilots participated in a 2,800-mile cross-country air derby. Participants included Pancho Barnes (left), Amelia Earhart (third from left), and Gladys O'Donell (with helmet on). **History Office, Air Force Flight Test Center**

Jimmy Angel (left), Richard Halliburton, Pancho Barnes, and Moye Stephens. Date unknown.
John W. Underwood Collection

in major air races. The next year she returned to the Powder Puff Derby in a new Travel Air *Mystery Ship*, in which she set a world's speed record for women flyers with an average speed of 196.19 miles per hour.

Not resting on her laurels, Pancho sought yet another outlet for her flying skills. She worked hard on her aerobatic flying and became one of Hollywood's high profile stunt pilots. Pancho was a double for Louise Fezenda in the horseback scenes in the early Rin Tin Tin movies. In her next challenge she was the technical director for Pathe's *The Flying Fool*.

Shortly after, she started her own company, hired three pilots, and talked the studios into contracting out stunt-flying rather than hiring pilots individually as they traditionally had done. As her reputation grew, so also did her social life. She befriended Gary Cooper, Tyrone Power, and Errol Flynn.

But the good life could not go on forever, and as Pancho's inheritance dwindled, the nation headed into the Depression. In 1935, she pooled all her remaining assets into a small ranch in the western Mojave Desert. Although she had left Hollywood behind and now worked cattle, hogs, and horses, Pancho always owned some kind of aircraft. She

Pancho Barnes enjoyed sponsoring local rodeos, even though she lost money. Big crowds attended the marathon parties, and one year a naked "Lady Godiva" appeared. History Office, Air Force Flight Test Center

soon built an airstrip on the ranch and invited her Hollywood friends to fly with her over the mountains for fun.

As fate would have it, her ranch was near Muroc, which was on the edge of Rogers Dry Lake, forty-four square miles of smooth hard lake bed. The U.S. Army Air Corps decided that this area was the perfect place for a bombing and gunnery range. Pancho cashed in on the new and expanding base by supplying pork and milk in exchange for garbage (which she used to feed her hogs).

She soon expanded her dairy operations, selling dairy products throughout the region, and improved her ranch by enlarging the ranch house and adding a swimming pool. The military kept expanding its population at Muroc Army Airfield. World War II fueled much of the expansion, and Pancho decided to be patriotic, so she invited off-duty pilots to drop by her ranch for a drink and a swim. Those who could ride were offered horses. Soon she hired attractive hostesses to serve dinner to the weary airmen. Eventually, the booming ranch was renamed the Happy Bottom Riding Club.

High-ranking officers (Jimmy Doolittle and General H. H. "Hap" Arnold, for example) started showing up at the ranch to enjoy Pancho's earthy hospitality. When the war was over, Muroc became Edwards Air Force Base. The air force then decided that Edwards would be perfect for an experimental flight test center. Veteran air force pilots like Chuck Yeager, Al Boyd, Pete Everest, and Jack Ridley moved to Edwards and started working on supersonic flights. In 1947, Yeager broke the sound barrier in the X-1. The pilots became regulars at Pancho's ranch, and she and Yeager formed a lifelong friendship. Yeager recalled in his autobiography that Gene May, a civilian test pilot, asked him and a fellow pilot whether the X-1 program would ever be successful. Pancho immediately jumped in. "That's right, Gene, these two can fly right up your ass and tickle your right eyeball, and you would never know why you were farting shock waves."[1] Another time Pancho wondered out loud how why Bob Hoover, also a test pilot, was only a lieutenant. She promptly picked up the phone and called General Carl Spaatz at his unlisted number in Washington, D.C. 'Tooey, I've got a young lieutenant here named Bob Hoover, who's being f—— over royally.' Hoover liked to have died, and I [Yeager] stopped laughing by the next day."[2]

Above, left: Pancho Barnes with one of her beloved pigs. She had her own dairy farm, hog, cattle and horse-breeding operations. She also owned a garbage-hauling business. History Office, Air Force Flight Test Center

Above, right: Pancho Barnes enjoyed playing bartender for military pilots. She especially enjoyed playing good-natured jokes on "greenhorn" pilots who had just transferred to Edwards Air Force Base. History Office, Air Force Flight Test Center

Pancho Barnes's 80-acre compound included an airstrip, guest ranch, dance hall, bar, and grill.
History Office, Air Force Flight Test Center

Nothing is permanent in military assignments, and Pancho's great business with the base diminished after 1952 when Yeager's boss, Colonel Albert Boyd, was promoted. He had been one of Pancho's supporters. The next base commander made many changes at Edwards Air Force Base. Eventually, the base expanded so much that Pancho's operation was in the way. And unlike the good old days, the new test pilots were not bachelors but rather the married variety who stayed home. Pancho's ranch was no longer a popular gathering place. The air force eventually condemned her property, as the runways were extended. To make matters worse, Pancho's ranch house burned down one night. Her great life was winding down in an unfortunate way. She moved away, survived two cancer operations, but died alone in 1975. But Pancho had the last word: "Well, —— it, we had more fun in a week than most of the weenies in the world have in a lifetime."[3]

Pancho has not been forgotten by those who serve at Edwards Air Force Base. An annual barbecue is held at the site of the Happy Bottom Riding Club in remembrance of her high flying days.

After 1945, most of Pancho Barnes's clients were test pilots at nearby Muroc Army Airfield in the Mojave Desert. Later, the field's name was changed to Muroc Air Force Base, and in 1949 it became Edwards Air Force Base. The original test pilot unit had 13 employees. By 1952, the number had grown to 196.
History Office, Air Force Flight Test Center

CHAPTER 10

Nick Lentine: The Zero-Zero Barnstormer

As a kid in New Jersey in the early 1920s, Nick Lentine always hung out at the Newark airport where he could watch the air mail pilots come and go around the clock. They were his heroes, and as he later said, "I marveled at them and knew I wanted to be just like them and learn to fly."[1]

In 1927, at age 20, Lentine moved from New York City to Pasadena, California, to learn to fly. The weather was certainly better for flying in southern California than in the East, and he found a job at the local airport that paid him $10 a week plus one hour of flight instruction. Eventually, he earned his pilot's license as well as his A&P (aircraft mechanic) license.

Nick Lentine was 96 in October 2004 when this photograph was taken at his favorite hangout, Porterville Municipal Airport in California. ©Bruce McAllister

Nick Lentine's business card from 1933. Note his three-digit telephone number. Courtesy Nick Lentine

During his early years as a pilot, Lentine organized three flying clubs; his first was called the Yellow Cab Flying Club, and he and his students jointly owned a Curtiss Jenny JN-4D. With high hopes for making it big in the expanding world of aviation, Lentine eventually saved up enough money to buy a Waco 10 biplane and began a fixed base operation (FBO) that included a flight school, charter service, and barnstorming. Word of Lentine's good reputation as an instructor and charter pilot spread in the Los Angeles area, and he landed a stunt-flying contract for a Will Rogers movie.

Nick Lentine (left) poses with stunt parachutist Tex Seaborn and his Curtiss Jenny JN-4D in 1928. At the time, Lentine was giving Seaborn flying lessons, although he had only 17 hours of flight time himself. Courtesy Bob Lentine

Opposite: Nick Lentine (right) was giving flying lessons to Kenny Bates in this Curtiss Jenny JN-4D when this photograph was taken in 1929. At the time, Nick was 19 and had about 150 hours of flight time. Courtesy Bob Lentine

Lentine also knew Howard Hughes and was given a contract in *Hell's Angels*, taxiing Fokker aircraft in ground scenes.

Fog was always a challenge for pilots in southern California, and Lentine made national headlines when he became the first pilot to ever land on a city street in Montrose, near Pasadena, on a foggy night—May 12, 1931.[2] A man had chartered Lentine to make a night flight to San Bernardino. What should have been a relatively short and uneventful $15 flight in a Travel Air biplane became a nightmare as they flew into a dense fog bank that had no top or no bottom. Just as the aircraft was running out of gas, Lentine saw some lights directly beneath the aircraft and promptly let down. They landed on Honolulu Street in Montrose, just missing some high-tension power lines and cutting some telephone lines. The next day, the CAA (now the FAA) looked over the impromptu airstrip and

Above: Will Rogers is making a quick exit from the aircraft in this scene from the movie Ambassador Bill. **Courtesy Bob Lentine**

Opposite: Will Rogers (left) with Nick Lentine in 1931 when they were filming Ambassador Bill. *Lentine was his pilot in the movie.* **Courtesy Bob Lentine**

checked out the aircraft for required night landing lights and compliance with other regulations. Luckily, Lentine had a tiny bicycle light on one strut that gave the CAA man an excuse to sign him off for a departure from Montrose's main street. Classes at the local school were cancelled, and all the school kids came out for the big sendoff. The police blocked the street and gave him permission to take off, minus his passenger, who had decided he'd had enough flying for a lifetime and took a streetcar home.

In the early 1930s, Lentine flew a photographer inside the Rose Bowl to capture the kickoff for the annual Bowl game. A CAA inspector attending the game "looked the other way." In those days, regulations were less often enforced—and inspectors had more leeway. Lentine also often flew photographers over businesses so they could take aerial photographs for advertising brochures.

One of Lentine's more famous students was Fresno-born Kirk Kerkorian, who also took up flying at an early age. Lentine recalled, "I lost track of Kirk for a few years, but a year or so after the war [World War II] I heard he was trying to fly gamblers from Los Angeles to Las Vegas."[3] That venture eventually turned into Western Airlines.

In 1940, Lentine helped design, develop, and operate the El Monte Airport east of Los Angeles where his flight school became part of the Civilian Pilot Training program. When World War II broke out, the government ordered the flight school to move 150 miles inland to Baker, near Death Valley, California. Soon the government shut down the cadet program, and Lentine quickly found a job as a Convair civilian test and ferry pilot in San Diego. There was a tremendous demand for pilots with his experience.

Lentine recalled ferrying the navy's Consolidated PB4Y-2 Privateer aircraft (the navy's four-engine version of the air force's Consolidated B-24 bomber) from San Diego to Litchfield, Arizona, where the manufacturer put guns on them. He remembered the PB4Y-2 to be a "sweet flying" air-

Opposite: Nick Lentine was flying a paying passenger in this Travel Air 4000 from Whittier, California, in the early 1930s when he had to make his famous landing through thick fog on the main street of Montrose, California. Courtesy Bob Lentine

craft. Unlike the air force version, the navy model had a single vertical stabilizer. Instructors liked to intimidate PB4Y-2 student pilots by pulling power on the number three engine just as the aircraft was rotating on takeoff.

After World War II, Lentine was employed as a flight instructor and as a pilot examiner for a few years before becoming a successful chicken farmer. In his retirement, Lentine likes to hang out at the Porterville, California, airport with his cronies. As he put it, "Flying is still in my blood, it really never leaves you. I know that as I marveled at the air mail pilots with their helmet and goggles when I was a child, I would do the same with the jet pilots and spacemen of today were I a child again, and follow the same path—skyward."[4]

Nick Lentine crashing a plane into a barn for a movie scene in 1932. **Courtesy Bob Lentine**

CHAPTER 11

Chuck Doyle: Minnesota Stuntman-Barnstormer

Living legend Charles P. "Chuck" Doyle is probably one of Minnesota's last surviving barnstormers and arguably its best. Born May 26, 1916, in Minneapolis, Doyle was the only son of an Irish plumber. At age 11, he bicycled to the Minneapolis airport to see Charles Lindbergh, just back from his historic trans-Atlantic flight. From that day on, Chuck was "hooked" on aviation and soon hitched a ride on a U.S. Navy aircraft. His father had swapped some plumbing work in exchange for the father and son getting individual rides in the navy trainer.

As a teenager, Doyle had an eye for the girls and often rode his motorcycle at high speeds around the streets of Minneapolis. But he was even more interested in becoming a hangar "rat" and spent much time around Wold-Chamberlain Field in Minneapolis. Soon he swapped his Harley Davidson Model 45 motorcycle and agreed to do some maintenance work without pay—in exchange for lessons in an OX-5-powered Waco 10 aircraft. Times were hard, and the cost for flying lessons was $7 an hour.

A few days after his sixteenth birthday in 1932, Doyle soloed after an hour and forty minutes of instruction from Bill Shaw who owned the Waco.[1] Doyle played football at Washburn High School, and soon an incident with his coach pushed him even further into his flying career. Incensed that the coach "grounded" him for an important game because he

---

Opposite: Chuck Doyle was 88 when this photograph was taken of him in Minneapolis. ©Bruce McAllister

had been late to a practice, Chuck borrowed an aircraft and made an extremely low-level pass right over the homecoming crowd. The school principal would not let the incident pass and expelled Doyle from Washburn High School. (Forty years later they finally gave him not one but two degrees to correct this snub.)

Chuck's first plane was an OX-5 Travel Air, which cost him $215. He took out a one-year loan to finance it. At the air shows, Chuck sold tickets for several "name" barnstormers. His typical commission was 10 cents a ticket—10 percent of a $1 ticket. (In those days, 10 cents would buy a hamburger.) He also did some parachuting at shows from 1935 to 1937. He would rent a parachute for $5 and pack it himself. As his market potential on the circuit improved, Doyle went to Hollywood where they were making Tom Mix movies, and he joined Bob Ward's flying circus. Doyle did everything—daredevil pilot routines, jumping from a motorcycle to an airplane, and parachuting. At the 1935 Minnesota State Fair, he jumped rows of cars with a specially equipped motorcycle.

Chuck also barnstormed in the Dakotas and was a partner in a crop-dusting business there. He

Chuck Doyle demonstrates his wing-walking routine for the photographer while a Travel Air 4000 aircraft does a static run-up. Date unknown. **Courtesy Chuck Doyle**

Captain Frank Frakes, expert house-crasher, posed for this publicity photo in front of a Challenger Robin in 1935. Courtesy Vern Georgia

Opposite: Frank "Bowser" Frakes enjoyed crashing into buildings such as this one at the 1935 Minnesota State Fair. He was flying a Waco 9 aircraft. The infield side of the building is open to help extricate the pilot more quickly after the crash. Courtesy Noel Allard

Chuck Doyle, performing the human battering-ram act, on the hood of what appears to be a 1937 Chevrolet sedan. A wooden framework just in front of his head gives him some protection from serious injury. Date unknown. Courtesy Chuck Doyle

did a little bit of everything with Mel Swanson, who later flew with him for Northwest Airlines. Swanson had to remind him not to jump out of the passenger aircraft they were flying for Northwest.

During his barnstorming days, Doyle twice crashed into houses—on purpose. The first crash was with Danny Fowlie at the State Fair. "We would construct the building so that it would stop [the plane] instantly. Two telephone poles would stop the plane in 10 feet—those fast stops [are] where we would get hurt. The next one we went through the entire building and stopped in 150 feet. That was safer and more spectacular. We would charge $500 for a house crash. We would buy an airplane for a couple of hundred bucks and we would get ten or twenty bucks for the plane after we had destroyed it.

We would have the state Fair Board build the house . . . we would have them throw that in."[2] Asked why he never got hurt, Chuck fired back, "I always landed on my head so that I would not get hurt."[3]

Doyle still has burn scars on his arms from driving a motorcycle through a tunnel of flames. He wore a leather jacket to cut exposure to the flames but admitted, "We would get a bit scorched. We got $40 for that act."[4]

For one season, Chevrolet sponsored the Bob Ward

Bob Ward's
Hollywood Aces
Minn State Fair 1937
Fowlie's House Crash

Bull's eye! Danny Fowlie crashing into a house at the 1937 Minnesota State Fair. **Courtesy Jim LaVake**

stunt show in which Doyle participated. The local dealer loaned them a Chevy, which they promptly trashed. The factory was alleged to be sending a new car to replace the one they crashed, but it never showed up and the local dealer went after the performers. Doyle and his partners left town in the middle of the night, headed for greener pastures in Florida.

Down south, however, business turned bad, and Bob Ward was thought to have absconded with all the money. Danny Fowlie and Doyle were left with hardly anything but a single-seat motorcycle. So they rented a room in a home for $1 (the going rate), had a good night's sleep, "borrowed" a couple of pillows for the motorcycle's passenger seat, and again took off in the middle of the night—this time with a soft ride. But luck was not on their side. They ran into a snowstorm, had to put the motorcycle in storage, and take a bus home. It had been a bad year, working for Captain Bob Ward and his Hollywood Daredevil Aces.

Doyle had other misadventures and money problems. Once he jumped out of Mel Swanson's Ford Tri-motor and landed on a roof at Fort Snelling near Minneapolis. "It was during the State

An unidentified pilot poses with his Waco 9 aircraft at Mayer, Minnesota, before it was flown into a house at an air show. The worn-out plane broke down several times en route to Mayer, hence the "Mayer or Bust" inscription on the aircraft. Courtesy Noel Allard

Fair and was to be the first double parachute jump—two people holding on to each other—me and Stella Kindle. We landed on the tile roof and cracked a tile. This fellow came up to me and wanted to know what my name was. It ended up that I got a bill for $12 or $14. Mel never remitted the money due."[5]

He recalled another incident. "I had done three or four parachute jumps at Fargo, North Dakota, and a CAA fellow came up to me and asked to look over my parachutes. He looked at them and then stated, 'I've known a lot of parachute jumpers but have not known them very long. Try them [the parachutes] and see if they work.' In those days we did not rehearse anything. We lost a few parachutists—one at the State Fair and one in the river—it took a couple of weeks to find the body of the one that landed in the river."[6]

Chuck built a tremendous reputation over the years buying and restoring exotic aircraft. He donated a replica of a 1910 Curtiss pusher that is on display at Gate 9 at the Minneapolis–St. Paul International Airport. It was flown in *The Great Race*, a 1965 movie, starring Tony Curtis. He also is the only person to have donated three aircraft to the Air Force Museum at Wright Patterson Air Force Base. They include the first North American A-36 Apache, a dive-bombing version of the P-51A Mustang, and a Curtiss P-40E. His hangars house many legendary aircraft, all of which had long and exciting histories. He still talks to Boy Scouts and students, exhorting them to get an education and perhaps pursue an aviation career. Chuck is proud of his membership in several aviation halls of fame, but perhaps his greatest honor was receiving an honorary degree from Washburn High School in 2002, sixty-eight years after he "buzzed" his schoolmates and was expelled.

Five-gallon cans and a horse-drawn wagon sometimes were the only way to deliver fuel to aircraft at remote fields used for barnstorming. Clarence Kvale is refueling the aircraft while Andrew Buhl (left), Paul Nalewaja, and a farmer supervise the operation. **Courtesy Ignatious Nalewaja**

CHAPTER 12

John Miller: The One-Minute Barnstormer

John M. Miller of Poughkeepsie, New York (age 98 in 2004), is one of the best-known living barnstormers in the United States. He soloed in his Curtiss Jenny on December 25, 1923, earned his airframe and engine certificate (to be an A&P mechanic) in 1927, and worked for the Gates Flying Circus in Pittsfield, Massachusetts, as a mechanic the same year.

After saving up some money, he bought a Standard J-1 aircraft, with a 180-horsepower Hisso engine upgrade. It took him six months to restore the aircraft. He hoped to cram four paying passengers in the front cockpit for barnstorming rides, but new regulations allowed only two. So, in 1929, he sold it in favor of the New Standard D-25 aircraft, with a Wright J-5 225-horsepower engine. He now had an aircraft that could carry four paying passengers, facing forward, in the front cockpit. He had a revolutionary idea for making barnstorming more profitable—better advertising and very short flights.

Former barnstormer John Miller, a lifelong resident of Spackenkill, New York, holds a brass model of a World War I French Spad fighter in front of his home. Miller soloed in his own Curtiss Jenny in 1923 and worked as a mechanic for the Gates Flying Circus in the late 1920s. He barnstormed in a Standard D-25 in the late 1920s and hauled as many as 200 passengers per hour. The New Standard could carry 4 passengers, and Miller pioneered very short rides that were cheaper and yet still increased his daily gross. ©Spencer Ainsley

John Miller poses for a photograph with his Curtiss Jenny JN-4 in 1924. John Miller/EAA Vintage Aircraft Association

He printed his promotional material on the blank side of penny postcards and mailed the cards to every post office box holder in an area on successive days about half a week before his flights. The cards hyped his wonderful new $10,000 plane, touted as the same kind that Charles Lindbergh flew across the Atlantic in 1927. He advertised rides—with "stunt" flying and dead-stick landings—for $1 per person. Local gas stations were offered the great privilege of having their logo painted on the side of the fuselage of the Standard (in washable watercolor) in exchange for two or three drums of Gulf or Texaco auto gasoline and some engine oil delivered to the site free.

When the cards showed up at farms and villages, the excited kids would talk their parents into taking them on Saturday or Sunday after they had done their chores.

Miller, a master of logistics, planned his flights to last exactly one minute. He would arrange with local farmers to clear a field so that the "run-

With engine running, John Miller refuels his New Standard aircraft while passengers climb on board. John Miller/EAA Vintage Aircraft Association

way" was long enough to enable him to take off in the same direction as he landed—without turning around or taxiing unnecessarily. While four passengers got into the Standard on one side, a member of his crew would help the previous flight's passengers disembark from the other side. Miller would stay in the cockpit for hours and for many flights (relieving himself with a homemade relief tube, drinking

John Miller was very successful barnstorming with this custom New Standard aircraft, Serial Number 2. It could carry 4 passengers in the front cockpit. After barnstorming slowed down in the 1930s, liquor smugglers used this plane to haul 1,000-pound loads of scotch whiskey from Canada into the United States. John Miller/EAA Vintage Aircraft Association

Officials, including Eddie Rickenbacker (third from left), give John Miller the first air mail to be carried by a Kellett KD-1 Autogiro. The 6-mile air mail route from the roof of the Philadelphia Post Office to the Philadelphia airport was the shortest airline route in the United States. This plane was also the first wingless aircraft to get certification before the advent of the helicopter. John Miller/EAA Vintage Aircraft Association

water, and snacking between flights). The engine would not be shut down between flights, and while passengers were embarking and disembarking, the plane would often be refueled.

Passengers rarely had time to get their seat belts on because the flights were so short. Miller noted that often he "was taking off before [the passengers] even had a chance to sit down."[1] In one hour Miller would usually complete about 50 flights. He easily made 250 to 350 flights per day, generating $1,000 to $1,400 in gross revenue.

The one-minute flights were quite simple. After liftoff into the wind, the plane was kept low for two or three seconds, allowing airspeed to build. Then Miller would climb into a combination wingover and Immelmann climbing turn. After passing the touchdown area on the downwind leg, Miller made a steep turn with a dramatic slip to final and touched down at the designated spot. The Standard's tailskid eventually dug a hole in the ground where it touched down repeatedly in precisely the same place.

These roller-coaster flights were an instant success, and some customers got right back in line for another flight. In later years, when Miller was an airline pilot, he recalled copilots and flight attendants asking him how he could make such great landings; he would simply reply that he'd had "a helluvalotta practice while barnstorming, like 250 or more landings a day."[2]

Miller was proud of his secret barnstorming techniques and stayed away from airports. He was always out working the farm country and never let on how many passengers he would carry each day. His competition was working the airports and taking passengers up for 10- to 15-minute rides. Little did they know about the one-minute barnstormer!

John Miller with the one-of-a-kind Kellett KD-1 Autogiro in which he carried the first air mail from the roof of the Philadelphia Post Office to the airport. **John Miller/EAA Vintage Aircraft Association**

CHAPTER 13

Jack Greiner: The Friendly Barnstormer

Jack Greiner, who celebrated his eighty-fourth birthday in 2004, still cherishes his days of barnstorming. He enjoys reminiscing with pilots who often fly their antique aircraft to the private airstrip in Longmont, Colorado, near Greiner's home. His eyes are edged with crow's-feet, showing the thousands of hours he has logged in all manner of aircraft—from DC-3s to Waco Straight Wing ASO biplanes. Jack was introduced to flying when he was hired to sell tickets for barnstormers in Minneapolis in 1933. By 1937, he had earned his pilot's license and had become a barnstormer. Eventually, he barnstormed in Missouri, Iowa, Wisconsin, and New Jersey.

Decades later, Jack eloquently articulated his love of barnstorming. "I don't know—it's different; the wind, noise and smell . . . old biplanes smell different than other airplanes, you know. It's the fabric and dope. And they sound different too. The wind in the wires, especially when the power is shut off. It's just different . . . there is nothing else like flying an open airplane with two wings . . . especially when she is big and red and beautiful."[1]

The attack on Pearl Harbor in December 1941 ended air shows abruptly, and Jack became a civilian instructor in the army's glider program for a brief period. Shortly thereafter, at age 21, he signed on with American Airlines and became an airline

---

Jack Greiner barnstorming near Sully, Iowa, in 1989 in his Waco Straight Wing ASO biplane. ©Mike Fizer

Jack Greiner in 1939, when he was working for George Bringhurst, maintaining some Cubs, a Stinson, a Fleet, and a Rearwin aircraft. His pay was 25 cents an hour, and on his free time, he earned a couple of hours of flight time every week. Courtesy Jack Greiner

Opposite: On the road with Jack Greiner and his home-built camper mounted on a 1930 Model A Ford. He lived in this vehicle in 1940 when he was barnstorming out of the Minneapolis airport. Courtesy Jack Greiner

Left: Jack Greiner ice-barnstorming off the Mississippi River, near Prescott, Wisconsin, in 1938. Courtesy Jack Greiner

Right: Jack Greiner (in lower Piper Cub) with his friend Danny Fowlie performing at an air show in the Midwest in 1941. The aircraft could not take off or land when they were in tandem as in this photograph. Courtesy Jack Greiner

captain at the age of 23; it was unusual at the time to achieve that position at such a young age. Before polio temporarily grounded him in 1953, Greiner had logged more than 8,000 hours in a DC-3 over a period of eight years.

In 1990, Greiner and his wife, June, took their 1930 Waco CTO Taperwing to Iowa where they followed a weeklong bike ride across the state. Whenever they could generate enough interest, they would land and give rides to the bikers. From there, the Greiners continued across Iowa, Nebraska, and Missouri, visiting about 40 towns and giving more than 1,000 rides a month.

Greiner claims that barnstorming today is much the same as it was 60 years ago. He and his wife are often invited to the home of someone from the town in which they are performing. "We land, and some farmer will see us and come and ask what he can do for us. We've stayed at people's houses and farms we don't even know. We seldom stay in a motel."[2] And if he uses a farmer's field, he makes the traditional offer of 5 percent of the take or offers free rides for the farmer's entire family. If he doesn't have somebody to sell tickets, he recruits a local kid who gets a 10 percent commission on every ticket sold. "I've even had a kid bring me 5-gallon cans of gas in his red wagon in exchange for a ride, just

Jack Greiner's official American Airlines portrait, taken in December 1942. He flew for American Airlines for 11 years before polio temporarily grounded him. Courtesy Jack Greiner

Opposite: Jack Greiner driving a Ford while his buddy Danny Fowlie lands a Piper Cub on top, December 7, 1941 (the day Japan bombed Pearl Harbor). It was his last air show in the Midwest before World War II. ***Courtesy*** Jack Greiner

Jack Greiner showing his ribbon-cutting routine at an air show in the Midwest, 1941. Courtesy Jack Greiner

Opposite: Jack Greiner with his wife, June, and their Waco QC F-2 aircraft in 1979. Courtesy Jack Greiner

like we did when we were kids."[3] Greiner prefers to visit towns that have grass strips or open fields and where a biplane's arrival is a big enough event to attract people and dogs. Sully, Iowa, is one of Greiner's favorite stops because it is a small farming community of just under 1,000 people and traditional values are still in place—doors are not locked and flags are out on all holidays. The windsock on the municipal grass strip proclaims: Iowa—A Place to Fly.

The income Greiner makes from barnstorming is secondary to him. By the time he calculates all his expenses, there is not much profit. Insurance and the cost of overhauling his biplane run up operating costs. "Most of the barnstormers I knew were just trying to meet costs to support their true love, building up their flying time to get a job with the airlines."[4]

Greiner's motivation to barnstorm comes mainly from the people he meets. He gets a kick out of people's reactions to the rides, noting that "you can almost read people's minds by the positions of their bodies, and communicate with them without words."[5] Greiner believes and hopes that barnstorming will not become a memory for the small towns of America. "There is a great nostalgia in our country for how it used to be and there are still a lot of places where, if you fly in with an antique biplane, they still give you the keys to the town."[6]

Jack Greiner(left) and Vearl Root during their 1990 barnstorming trip at Sully, Iowa. Their Waco YKS-7 aircraft is on the right and a Waco ATO Taperwing aircraft on the left.
©*Mike Fizer*

Jack Greiner in June 2004.
©*Bruce McAllister*

CHAPTER 14

Charlie Kulp: The Flying Farmer

Charlie Kulp, born in 1925 and known to many North American aviation fans as the Flying Farmer, has put on his aerial circus more than 800 times in the past 31 years. Averaging approximately 35 performances a year, this Virginia-based modern-day barnstormer demonstrates an uncanny knack of pushing his aircraft's outer envelope and defying gravity in his aerial stunts. He dazzles crowds with his demonstrations of "how not to fly" an aircraft and is the perfect "bungling" farmer in the unique show. His long beard and tattered farmer garb add spice to the hilarious air show.

When asked how much he practices, he replied, "Practice? Ruin my routine?"[1] His great sense of humor and the sight of him in his little yellow plane have helped this seemingly inept farmer-pilot captivate his audiences with thrills and aerial spills. He never flies higher than 600 feet above the ground in his routines, which means his spins and loops begin at 600 feet or lower, not giving him any margin for error. Both buildings and spectators can limit his options to correct for drift and often "box" him in. So he flies on a wing and a prayer, realizing that he can't really "see" up and down drafts as he does his routines at extremely low altitudes.

His show aircraft is a standard 65-horsepower Piper J-3 Cub—unmodified since it was manufactured in 1946. Thousands have learned to

Charlie Kulp with his favorite stunt plane, the Piper J-3. Courtesy Charles Kulp

Charlie Kulp (left) and his brother Harry in front of an Aeronca C-3 aircraft in the late 1940s.
Courtesy Charles Kulp

Charlie Kulp "storms" away from his Piper J-3 Cub after performing his patented Flying Farmer act.
Courtesy Charles Kulp

fly in the Piper basic trainer, which was manufactured before and after World War II; many barnstormers like its versatility for putting on aerial stunts.

Although most of Kulp's shows are in the United States, including appearances at major events such as Oshkosh and Sun 'n' Fun, he has also appeared at civilian and military air shows in Great Britain and Canada. When he is not on the road, he does Sunday afternoon shows at his home-base airstrip in Bealeton, Virginia.

In addition to his air shows, Kulp works as an FAA-certified flight instructor, and in the fall of 2000 he received the coveted Charles Taylor Award from the FAA for his 50 years of work as an A&P mechanic. In 1997, he was inducted into the Virginia Aviation Hall of Fame—not bad for a "bungling" barnstormer!

Charlie Kulp preparing to fly a Beachey Looper replica in 1971. The aircraft was powered by an 80-horsepower LeRhone rotary engine. Courtesy Charles Kulp

Opposite: Charlie Kulp taught stunt-flying to the Randall brothers. Courtesy Charles Kulp

Notes

Introduction

1. Jack Greiner interview by Bruce McAllister, September 16, 2004.
2. Don Dwiggins, *The Barnstormers*, p. 110.
3. David H. Onkst, U.S. Centennial of Flight Commission Web site.
4. Charles Lindbergh, *WE*, p. 58.
5. Ibid., p. 60.
6. K. C. Tessendorf, *Barnstormers and Daredevils*, p. 51.

Chapter 1

1. Curtis Prendergast, *Epic of Flight Series—The First Aviators*, pp. 143–144.
2. *Flight Journal*, April 1999, p. 42.
3. Frank Marrero, *Lincoln Beachey: The Man Who Owned the Sky*, p. 177.
4. Ibid., p. 82.

Chapter 2

1. Don Dwiggins, *The Barnstormers*, p. 77.
2. Martin Caidin, *Barnstorming*, p. 78.
3. Don Dwiggins, *The Barnstormers*, p. 112.

Chapter 3

1. Don Dwiggins, *The Barnstormers*, p. 110.
2. Bill Rhode, *Chewing Gum, Bailing Wire & Guts*, p. 15.
3. Carl Cleveland, *Upside-Down Pangborn*, p. 54.
4. Bill Rhode, *Chewing Gum, Bailing Wire and Guts*, p. 185.

Chapter 4

1. H. Hugh Wynne, *The Motion Picture Stunt Pilots*, p. 38.
2. Walt and Ann Bohrer, *Tales Up!* p. 119.
3. Ibid., p. 119.
4. William Goldman, *The Great Waldo Pepper*, p. 222.
5. Ibid., p. 223.
6. Frank Tallman, *Flying the Old Planes*, p. 140.

Chapter 5

1. Ernie Boffa interview by Bruce McAllister, January 2, 2002.
2. Z. Lewis Leigh, *And I Shall Fly*, p. 9.

Chapter 6

1. Ira Harkey, *Pioneer Bush Pilot*, p. 29.
2. Jean Potter, *The Flying North*, p. 83.
3. Ibid., p. 84.
4. Richard Wien letter to author, October 28, 2004.
5. Ibid., p. 85.

Chapter 7

1. Harry E. Mendenhall, *State House News: State House Employees Weekly* (Lincoln, NE), May 3, 1940: 1 (Diane Bartels Collection).

Chapter 8

1. *Frontier Airlines Magazine*, Fall, 1975, p. 30.
2. *Los Angeles Times*, May 25, 1980.
3. *Rapid City Journal*, May 8, 1969, p. 3.
4. *Los Angeles Times*, May 25, 1980, p. 14.

Chapter 9

1. Chuck Yeager and Leo Janos, *Yeager*, p. 139.
2. Ibid., p. 139.
3. Edwards AFB Web site, Florence Pancho Barnes Biography.

Chapter 10

1. *Fresno Bee,* August 24, 1995, p. SV1.
2. Ibid.
3. Ibid.
4. Ibid., p. SV4.

Chapter 11

1. Chuck Doyle interview by Terry Love in 2004.
2. Chuck Doyle interview by Bruce McAllister, June 16, 2004.
3. Ibid.
4. Ibid.
5. Ibid.
6. Ibid.

Chapter 12

1. John Miller telephone interview by Bruce McAllister, September 20, 2004.
2. *Vintage Airplane,* August 2003, p. 27.

Chapter 13

1. *Boulder Daily Camera FOCUS,* October 7, 1973, pp. 9–11.
2. *Wausau Daily Herald,* October 9, 1987.
3. *AOPA PILOT,* June 1993, p. 50.
4. Ibid., p. 51.
5. Ibid.
6. Ibid.

Chapter 14

1. Letters from Charlie Kulp to Bruce Mc Allister, 2004.

Bibliography

BOOKS

Allard, Noel, and Gerald Sandvick, *Minnesota Aviation History: 1857–1945.* MAHB Publishing Company, P.O. Box 284, Chaska, MN 55318, 1993

Autry, Peyton, *Reflections of a Teenage Barnstormer.* Turner Publishing, Paducah, KY, 2002

Bach, Richard, *The Bridge Across Forever.* Dell Publishing, New York, 1984

Bach, Richard, *A Gift of Wings.* Dell Publishing, New York, 1974

The Barnstormers—Pioneers of the Skies (DVD/Video), Up in the Air Pictures, 712 North Piedra Road, Sanger, CA 93657, 2002

Bartels, Diane Ruth Armour, *Sharpie—The Life Story of Evelyn Sharp.* Dageforde Publishing, Lincoln, NE, 68510, 1996

Bohrer, Walt and Ann, *Tales Up!* Aero Publishers, Fallbrook, CA, 1971

Boyne, Walter J., *Trophy for Eagles.* Crown Publishers, New York, 1989

Caidin, Martin, *Barnstorming.* Duell, Sloan & Pearce, New York, 1965

Cleveland, Carl M., *Upside-Down Pangborn—King of the Barnstormers.* Aviation Book Company, Glendale, CA, 1978

Dwiggins, Don, *The Barnstormers.* Grosset & Dunlap, New York, 1968

Ellis, Frank H., *Canada's Flying Heritage.* University of Toronto Press, Toronto, 1954

Gann, Ernest K., *Blaze of Noon.* Henry Holt, New York, 1946

Goldman, William (screenplay), based on a story by George Roy Hill, *The Great Waldo Pepper.* Dell Publishing, New York, 1975

Gowans, Bruce W., *Wings Over Lethbridge.* Historical Society of Alberta, Lethbridge, AB, Canada, 1986

Grant, R. G., *Flight—100 Years of Aviation.* Smithsonian/DK Publishing, New York, 2002

Harkey, Ira, *Pioneer Bush Pilot.* University of Washington, Seattle, WA, 1974

Hatfield, D. D., *Pioneers of Aviation*. Northrup University Press, Inglewood, CA, 1976

Homan, Lynn, and Thomas Reilly, *Wings Over Florida*. Arcadia Publishing, Charleston, SC, 1999

Kessler, Laura, *The Happy Bottom Flying Club—The Life and Times of Pancho Barnes*. Random House, New York, 2000

Kisor, Henry, *Flight of the Gin Fizz*. Basic Books, New York, 1997

Leary, William M. (editor), *Aviation's Golden Age—Portraits from the 1920s and 1930s*. University of Iowa, Iowa City, IA, 1989

Leigh, Z. Lewis, *And I Shall Fly*. CANAV Books, Toronto, Ontario, 1985

Lindbergh, Charles, *WE*. Grosset & Dunlap, New York, 1927

Marrero, Frank, *Lincoln Beachey—The Man Who Owned the Sky*. Scottwell Associates, San Francisco, 1997

Mohler, Stanley, and Bobby Johnson, *Wiley Post, His Winnie Mae, and the World's First Pressure Suit*. Smithsonian Institution Press, Washington, DC, 1971

Neely, William, *PILOTS: The Romance of the Air: Pilots Speak About the Triumphs and Tragedies, Fears and Joys of Flying*. Simon & Schuster, New York, 1991

O'Neil, Paul, *Epic of Flight Series—Barnstormers and Speed Kings*. Time-Life Books, Alexandria, VA, 1981

Potter, Jean, *The Flying North*. Curtis Publishing, New York, 1945

Prendergast, Curtis, *Epic of Flight Series—The First Aviators*. Time-Life Books, Alexandria, VA, 1981

Rhode, Bill, *Chewing Gum, Bailing Wire and Guts—The Story of the Gates Flying Service*. Kennikat Press, Port Washington, NY, 1970

Rickenbacker, Eddie V., *Fighting the Flying Circus*. Avon Books, New York, 1965

Salut, Harold, *Fragile Wings and Gentle Giants*. Blackbird Press, Dubuque, IA, 1985

Sedgwick, Rhonda, *Sky Trails—The Life of Clyde W. Ice*. Quarter Circle A Enterprises, 1159 State Hwy. 450, Newcastle, WY, 82701, 1988

Tallman, Frank, *Flying the Old Planes.* Doubleday, New York, 1973

Tessendorf, K. C., *Barnstormers and Daredevils.* Atheneum/MacMillan, New York, 1988

Thomas, Lowell, and Thomas, Lowell, Jr., *Famous Flights that Changed History.* Doubleday, Garden City, NY, 1968

Vecsey, George, and George Dade, *Getting Off the Ground— The Pioneers of Aviation Speak for Themselves.* E. P. Dutton, New York, 1979

Whitehouse, Arch, *The Early Birds.* Doubleday, New York, 1965

Whyard, Florence, *Ernie Boffa—Canadian Bush Pilot.* Beringian Books, Whitehorse, Yukon, 1984

Wohl, Robert, *A Passion for Wings.* Yale University Press, New Haven, CT, 1994

Wynne, H. Hugh, *The Motion Picture Stunt Pilots and Hollywood's Classic Aviation Movies.* Pictorial Histories Publishing Company, Missoula, MT, 1987

Yeager, Chuck, and Leo Janos, *Yeager—An Autobiography.* Bantam Books, New York, 1985

MAGAZINES & ARTICLES

AOPA PILOT, "Barnstormers," June 1993, pp. 43–53

Boulder Daily Camera FOCUS, October 7, 1973, pp. 9–11

Flight Journal, "The Forgotten Father of Aerobatics," April 1999, pp. 40–48

Fresno Bee, "Valley Man Earns Respect as Pilot, Chicken Rancher," August 24, 1995, pp. SV1, SV4

Frontier Airlines Magazine, "The Man Who Flew for Half a Century," Fall 1975, pp. 30–33

Los Angeles Times, "Clyde Ice, 90, Is Back with Spring Thaw," May 25, 1980, pp. 13–15

Rapid City Journal, "Still Dusting Crops at Age 80, Clyde Ice Remembers His First Flight 50 Years Ago," May 8, 1969, p. 3

Vintage Aircraft, "My Secret Barnstorming System Revealed," August 2003, pp. 4–6, 27

Wausau Daily Herald, "Antique Plane Lands in Ringle," October 9, 1987

The aircraft in the background (courtesy of Dan Murray, Longmont, Colorado) is a beautifully restored 1928 J-5 Travel Air Model 4000, with a 7-cylinder Wright "Whirlwind" engine.
©Brian Patarich

About the Author

A longtime resident of the Colorado Rockies, Bruce McAllister is a pilot, photographer, and writer who has logged many of his 4,900 hours of flight time in Alaska and Canada. His previous books are *Wings Across America, Wings Above the Arctic, Wings Over the Alaska Highway,* and *Wings Over Denali.*